M000273121

MADE
FOR
EDEN

Promises and Provisions for the
Life God Created You to Live

BY
DR. BRYAN MCINTOSH

IRON
STREAM

Birmingham, AL

Iron Stream
An imprint of Iron Stream Media
100 Missionary Ridge
Birmingham, AL 35242
IronStreamMedia.com

Copyright © 2022 by Bryan McIntosh
All rights reserved. First printing 2021.
Printed in the United States of America

Cover design by Hannah Linder

No part of this publication may be reproduced, stored in a retrieval system, or transmitted in any form or by any means—electronic, mechanical, photocopying, recording, or otherwise—without the prior written permission of the publisher.

Iron Stream Media serves its authors as they express their views, which may not express the views of the publisher.

Library of Congress Control Number: 2021944827

All scripture quotations, unless otherwise indicated, are taken from the Holy Bible, Unless otherwise noted, all Scripture quotations are taken from the Holman Christian Standard Bible®, Used by Permission HCSB ©1999,2000,2002,2003,2009 Holman Bible Publishers. Holman Christian Standard Bible®, Holman CSB®, and HCSB® are federally registered trademarks of Holman Bible Publishers.

Scriptures marked NKJV are taken from the NEW KING JAMES VERSION (NKJV): Scripture taken from the NEW KING JAMES VERSION®. Copyright© 1982 by Thomas Nelson, Inc. Used by permission. All rights reserved.

Scripture quotations marked TPT are from The Passion Translation®. Copyright © 2017, 2018 by Passion & Fire Ministries, Inc. Used by permission. All rights reserved. ThePassionTranslation.com.

Scriptures marked ESV are taken from the THE HOLY BIBLE, ENGLISH STANDARD VERSION (ESV): Scriptures taken from THE HOLY BIBLE, ENGLISH STANDARD VERSION * Copyright© 2001 by Crossway, a publishing ministry of Good News Publishers. Used by permission.

Scripture quotations marked MSG are taken from THE MESSAGE, copyright © 1993, 2002, 2018 by Eugene H. Peterson. Used by permission of NavPress, represented by Tyndale House Publishers. All rights reserved.

Scriptures marked NIV are taken from the NEW INTERNATIONAL VERSION (NIV): Scripture taken from THE HOLY BIBLE, NEW INTERNATIONAL VERSION *. Copyright© 1973, 1978, 1984, 2011 by Biblica, Inc.™. Used by permission of Zondervan.

Scriptures marked NAS are taken from the NEW AMERICAN STANDARD (NAS): Scripture taken from the NEW AMERICAN STANDARD BIBLE®, copyright© 1960, 1962, 1963, 1968, 1971, 1972, 1973, 1975, 1977, 1995 by The Lockman Foundation. Used by permission.

ISBN-13:   978-1-64526-325-8
eBook ISBN: 978-1-64526-326-5

1 2 3 4 5--26 25 24 23 22

Praise for *Made for Eden*

"Humanity traces its origin to God's good creation in the garden of Eden. Most folks don't know, however, that God's people are headed towards a renewed Eden that far surpasses the first. Bryan McIntosh is a trusted biblical scholar and clear writer whose life reflects the doctrine he professes. I can't think of a more helpful and encouraging guidebook for Christians to understand their amazing journey to a renewed Eden."

-Robert L. Plummer, Ph.D. *Collin and Evelyn Aikman Professor of Biblical Studies Chairman, New Testament Department,* The Southern Baptist Theological Seminary Author, *40 Questions about Interpreting the Bible*

"The Garden of Eden isn't primarily a place of bad news. It provides a glimpse of glory. In *Made for Eden,* Bryan McIntosh opens the door to one of our most basic longings – a place called home. Open these pages and join the journey to the destination God has prepared for you."

-Robert Whitlow, Best-selling author of *Chosen People*

"We all know what it's like to drift off course. In today's world, millions of Christians have faith in God, but live a life of aimless wandering. One reason for this is they have no clear vision for the life God intends for His children. In *Made For Eden,* Bryan McIntosh blows away the typical fog of confusion about life to reveal dynamic truth from God's Word that will empower you to recognize and walk in your divine destiny! A whole new life is waiting for you!"

-Greg Davis, Lead Pastor of Cornerstone Church, Southaven, Mississippi

"The Word of God clearly reveals we are living well below what God originally intended for us from the beginning. Now, through redemption, we are able to be "Partakers of the divine nature (see 2 Peter 1:4)." We need to have transformative thinking through the Holy Spirit in order to fulfills God's purpose. Bryan McIntosh has accomplished this task in his new book, *Made for Eden*. Bryan correctly states that, "Being made in the likeness of God carries a responsibility to carry out His purposeful design for our dominion over creation. That design is for us to function as the highest order of creation, and as image bearers, to exercise His authority."

I know you will be changed by this exceptional work. Enjoy!
-Kevin L. Zadai, Th. D. *Best selling author,*
Founder and President of Warrior Notes, and
Warrior Notes School of Ministry

"With precision and passion, crafted from years of study and personal pursuit, and investing in the lives of many, *Made for Eden* winsomely guides us on a journey to recover the greatest treasure of our God-bathed, God-initiated, and God-breathed reality, through grasping the depth and breadth of the Gospel."

Morgan Snyder
Author, Becoming a King
Founder, BecomeGoodSoil.com
Vice President, WildatHeart.org

"In *Made for Eden*, Bryan McIntosh paints a beautiful portrait of man as a new creation in Christ, fulfilling the purposes of God by God's power. Filled with hope, McIntosh reminds us that God not only restores man to His purpose through the cross, but He will also accomplish the future restoration of all things. I highly recommend this read!»

Becky Harling, Conference speaker and Best-selling author of *How to Listen So People Will Talk* and *The Extraordinary Power of Praise*

"The Bible opens with the beauty of creation and ends with the promise of a new creation, but we inhabit the messy in-between. Left to our own devices, we will attempt to fix our world by our own power, but the reality of what awaits us through God's restoration of the universe overwhelms the deepest of imaginations. Bryan McIntosh takes us on a tour of these biblical truths and reveals the unshakable hope of what is ahead as we refocus our sight upon eternity. Every exile from Eden should read this book!"

- Dustin C. George, Lead Pastor of Easthaven Baptist Church, Brookhaven, Mississippi

Dedication

To my wife Lynn and daughters Sarah and Ann, in whom I see the marvelous design God had for the feminine heart. Thank you for modeling it with grace, strength, and love. You are a reminder that God's purposes for the family are a great gift, a picture of His love for us. Thank you for bringing balance and joy to my life, as God meant for Adam to have with Eve, and means for all those after them to enjoy. I am so thankful for your love for Jesus and for others.

And to my parents, Jim and Helen McIntosh, for fostering opportunities for me to grow in life and in spirit, and for showing me at an early age that God's Word is to be treasured, known, and taken into the heart. Thank you, Mom and Dad, and also my parents-in-law, Bill and Judy Adams, for showing the generous, loving heart of the Father, and for modeling marriage so well for so long. I am blessed by each of you.

Acknowledgements

This book was years in the making, and as with any new endeavor, you learn as you go. Many people influenced me in the process.

Thank you to each of the women in my family. Thank you for the love and support, and for displaying mercy, hospitality, generosity, and faith.

Thank you to the men in my family, for showing me how to lead a family well, and how to apply that to shepherding God's people. Special thanks to my brother-in-law David Adams for the conversations through the years about our life with God, and for encouraging me to look with new perspective on His truth and apply it.

Thank you to the men I've been in close friendship with through the years. There are many of you, for reasons and in seasons. But I am a stronger believer in Jesus because of you.

Thank you to the pastors, professors, prophetic leaders, and lifelong friends who helped me see God's promises can be trusted, and that a life with faith as its foundation is worth pursuing. Each of you fostered my love for the Word.

Thank you to my sister and agent Blythe McIntosh Daniel, for encouraging me to write, and believing that it would be worth publishing. Thank you for reading part of the early work, helping me craft what was in my heart to say. And thanks to Art Daniel for supporting her work with authors which benefits many people.

Thank you to my publisher, Straight Street Books and Iron Stream Media, for believing in this topic and for publishing a first-time author.

Thank you to my editors, Amberlyn Dwinnell and Cindy Sproles, for helping me craft the message in order to say it clearly. I know the book is better because of your input.

To God the Father, Son, and Holy Spirit, this work is a result of the illumination You gave me about Your design for mankind and the relationship You meant us to enjoy with You when You made us in Your image. Thank You for the incredible honor You placed on us in appointing us to rule over Your creation and as Your ambassadors of restoration to a watching world.

Table of Contents

1

The Case for Eden

If we are honest, we all want to be important to someone. We want to know our life matters, that we are on earth for a purpose. We want that purpose to have significance, so when our life is over, the people who memorialize us will have something to say. For those who believe God created us, the question of "why was I made?" naturally arises. We want to believe our presence on earth is due to more than chance. Maybe the question comes as we enter adolescence, when we wish we were smarter or taller or more popular. Maybe our evaluation of our purpose comes as we search for our calling in life, or when we choose to give our life to another in marriage. Whenever this question comes, if we believe we are created by God, then success in our purpose is not measured by human definitions. Ultimately, the purpose we are made for can only be established by the One who made us. How well are we doing in the purpose in which our Creator says we should succeed? From the earliest pages of the Bible, God had a purpose in creating mankind. "Let us make mankind in our image, according to our likeness."[1] We were created as a reflection of the Divine. God gave us a responsibility: to rule over creation! We were made to steward what belongs to God. We were Made for Eden.

I believe this truth that we are made for Eden is overlooked. One reason for that is the focus in the story of creation swiftly shifts to one man's sin which separates him from God. And that sin also separated man from the environment where he was made to carry out his responsibility. But the original purpose of God for their lives remains true for ours. How do we engage with this very important role we were given: to reflect God's image and to rule over what He has given us? How do we gauge success in that role appropriately without thinking that success is based on our self-efforts?

If we better understood the connection between the creation of mankind and the final redemption, we would see how God made us to steward all He made. Jesus came as a man and lived a sinless life so He could redeem us to the role God gave man at creation. The return of Jesus, and the revelation of the New Heaven and New Earth are still future. In our day, the Father is still bringing to Himself the harvest of souls, until the gospel is preached to all.

This means the work for mankind to fulfill the purpose of God is still going on! Just as Adam and Eve had a job to do, so do we who follow Jesus. Rediscovering our role would give us hope for the future and excitement for the present. Far too many of us, instead of living with hope and excitement, carry around the weight of our circumstances, and that weight can erode the peace, joy, and vibrancy of faith that knowing our purpose should produce. God's redemptive story says we should have great hope, for His disciples will reign with Him over the creation like Adam and Eve in Eden.

To accelerate the coming of that future, Jesus tells us to pray that His will be done "on earth as it is in heaven."[2] We were made to bring heaven's will to earth, and through prayer we can see that happen. God honors this prayer for His will to be done through us because, at creation, He established our role as His agents. Jesus thought it necessary to tell us to pray this way because some people may believe the lie that what Adam and Eve lost can never be regained, that God's plan for mankind was irreparably altered by the sin in Eden. If we believe we can't return to our created purpose and therefore

2

can't fulfill the original mandate God gave us, to spread the truth of His goodness, what are we left with for our days on earth? If we can't be effective in what we were designed to do, why would we pray to see His will done here as in heaven as Jesus tells us to in the Lord's Prayer? In that prayer, it sounds like Jesus assigns us a part to play in seeing His will done on earth. And in fact, He does! But if any believe God's purpose for us was lost, then the best the believer can hope for in the midst of a sinful world is to be taken out of this world and "go to heaven."

The command of Jesus, and the example of Paul, is not to wait for an *escape to the afterlife* as our main pursuit while on earth. They both spoke of living water, of "resurrection and the life," of an overcoming life, and of the fulfillment of the "greater works" Jesus says we will do. They don't just advise waiting to be taken up into the clouds. There is a job to do while here. Paul says men are God's workmanship, the canvas upon which God produces His greatest work. Paul also teaches that God's will is accomplished as we each individually, as His workmanship, do the works He prepared for us before we ever embraced Him as our Redeemer. Not only are God's plans for mankind not lost, but He actually sees us as stewards of those plans, and intends for us to be busy carrying them out until He returns. What He began with Adam and Eve, He continues with us today.

Does being made for Eden mean we can experience the same intimacy with God that Adam and Eve had? God's favor and provision, such as a Father gives to a child, is enough to help us succeed in our purpose. The New Testament says He gives us all we need to succeed at what He means for us to do for Him.[3] We receive His guidance as well as the strength to obey that guidance through the life of God inside us. We receive His power through our dependence on His Spirit.[4]

The premise of this book is that man is created in God's image, and despite sin's entrance into the world, he becomes a new creation in Christ when redeemed by Him unto God's purpose. Through this reality of "new creation," we live out God's purpose through God's power as His messengers on this earth. This promise is expressed consistently from Genesis to Revelation. In fact, it is modeled in God's faithfulness to His people Israel in the Old Covenant and finds its completion in the gospel of the kingdom that Jesus announced and Paul embraced. While our sinful condition has affected our ability to fulfill the purpose of God for mankind, that purpose has never changed. We are designed to be His stewards and rulers over all creation. Because of Adam's sin, and the penalty it placed us under, the Father sent Jesus to earth in order to buy us back. In buying us back, we were transferred from Satan's domain and freed from sin and death. By this transfer of kingdoms, we once again belong to God and His rule and will be restored to the perfect environment God intended for us. The final book of the Bible, Revelation, is evidence that our "ruling" function among God's creation remains here on earth. We were made for Eden's perfection, and we were made to rule over all that God created in Eden.

How is our ruling role preserved and restored? Jesus' life, death, and resurrection removed the barrier sin created between mankind and God. Paul preached fully and clearly the reconciliation through Jesus' righteousness applied to us. Paul said this reconciliation restores our purpose as a "set-apart" people, through whom God shows His nature and His promises to those who have not believed.

Being "Made for Eden" means God not only restores men to His purpose, but He will also accomplish the future restoration of all things. Jesus lived with knowledge of the Father's purpose for Him during His time on earth. Jesus also demonstrated that He could live by the Father's direction.

The Apostle Paul also knew he was made to follow the voice of God. Paul understood his life's purpose would be fulfilled in becoming a new creation, re-birthed by God. Because this reality is available to all who believe, the message that we are Made for Eden is part of the gospel we must preach, it is truly "good news." Along these lines, this book has several conclusions I hope to support, in order to persuade readers of the truth of this "good news."

First, disciples of Jesus should be reminded of the glorious purpose God had for mankind when He created Adam and Eve, and even after their sin, of His promises to their descendants. We fulfill our purpose through the promise of His presence working in us.

Second, Jesus' death in obedience to the Father's plan is the key to our restoration to His purpose, and to our future with our Creator in the New Heaven and New Earth. Because in that death, we die with Him and will be raised with Him! Our old identity is crucified, and we receive a promised new life.

Third, Paul describes the new life that the crucified and risen Jesus produces in and for His disciples. He demonstrates how the Eden kind of life is renewed in us by the power of the Holy Spirit working inside us.

Fourth, the faithfulness of Jesus, shown in His obedience to the Father's will, provides us a restored relationship with the Father. We find our purpose in His love, and the salvation His obedience secures for us is the door to restoration to our created purpose. Our relationship with the Father is a privilege of walking closely to the Master as His stewards.

Finally, by viewing our life as new "in Christ," built to serve the kingdom Jesus rules as King, we receive the power needed to fulfill what God promised to Adam and Eve. The life of Jesus in us, the strength His power supplies, is the better, "New" Covenant. It is how we fulfill the purpose we were made for. Not only does that new life restore our original purpose, but we are given the power to fulfill that purpose!

This book is a study of a biblical theme. But it is one that also tells a story, starting in Genesis in the Garden of Eden, and ending in Revelation, with a garden on the new earth, both containing a tree of life. My aim is to make clearer the greatest true story ever told of a God who creates, rescues, redeems, restores, and resurrects a people for His own glory. We must be reminded that the story began in Eden with God's presence among men. The completion of the story in Revelation once again reflects the absence of sin and the presence of God among His people, the stewards over creation who serve Him. It is the story of people who willingly choose to be used and empowered by Him to achieve His purposes on the earth and whose goal is "as in heaven, so on earth."[5]

The Continuing Story of Being God's Possession

From the time God created mankind, He made Himself known to the people He called for His purposes. We read throughout Genesis about God's desire to save Noah and his family from the destruction by flood, to preserve righteous people and His purpose for all mankind. His relationships with Abraham and Isaac, Joseph, Moses, Joshua, the prophets, and kings are all evidence that God never gave up on His purposes for man. Through each figure in His story, God shows that He intends His people to serve His purposes. He says this through Moses on Mount Sinai. Exodus 19 says "'Now then, if you will indeed obey My voice and keep My covenant, then you shall be My own possession among all the peoples, for all the earth is Mine; and you shall be to Me a kingdom of priests and a holy nation.' These are the words that you shall speak to the sons of Israel."[6] And the elders of the people assure Moses they will do all the Lord has spoken. Yet Israel's history shows they did not faithfully keep this covenant, nor obey His voice.

But that promise of God's own being holy unto Him was not lost despite their disobedience to covenant. Peter, centuries later, understands that being included in God's family establishes us as set apart for God's purpose. He applies the Old Testament promise, spoken to Moses for Israel, that His gentile children serve Him as His own. Peter believes that the gentiles' inclusion among those who are set apart is a fulfillment of that promise in Exodus of being God's possession.[7]

The price for inclusion among God's own people was not silver or gold but was Jesus, a perfect sacrifice for all mankind. Through His death and resurrection, a new and living way of relating to God was established.

Peter's application of the promise of Exodus 19 to the gentiles is important because *the intent for which God set apart His people for His purposes still existed in the days Jesus was on earth.* God set Israel apart from the nations, to represent Him on earth. Yet their effectiveness in demonstrating God's character and His plans for His people was hindered by their disobedience and idolatry. The fulfillment of God's people serving His original purpose awaited the arrival of Messiah whose *life* would model the relationship with God that God intended with Israel. And His *death* would remove the barrier to *having* that relationship. Once the barrier was removed, God could bring into covenant with Himself men and women who received "sonship."

Life as "set apart people," as sons and daughters, has both privileges and responsibilities, as that act of redemption by Jesus was a purchase by God of our very lives. *The privilege is that the Godhead lives His life inside of us. The responsibility is to live as though we are His, because in fact we are.*[8] Because He purchased our redemption, the life we live is not our own. As Paul describes in Romans and in Galatians, when we are redeemed, we are "joining ourselves to God." We are to die with Him so we will be raised with Him, and we inherit all things with Jesus because of His obedience to His Father's will. We exercise our faith in offering ourselves to Him, as we make ourselves a living sacrifice.[9]

To become sons and daughters requires an act of faith. Jesus restores our life to God's design through living His life within us, so that we experience the life He made us for. Jesus is the first example of living this life. Paul calls him the firstborn of all creation, meaning not only is He the foremost among all men created, but He is the first to display the life that all children of God were meant to enjoy.[10]

Being Made for Eden Means Longing for the Divine

The depth with which we understand we are Made for Eden is reflected in what we wish for, and what we set our hope on. In his essay on hope in *Mere Christianity*, Lewis says the world educates us to fix our minds on this world, such that when the real desire for heaven is present in us, we don't recognize it. We want something this world cannot provide, and things the world offers "never quite keep their promise. The longings which arise in us when we first fall in love, or first think of some foreign country, or first take up some subject that excites us, are longings which no marriage, no travel, no learning, can really satisfy."[11] There is a wrong and a right way to handle this reality.

One "wrong" way is to think that another human relationship or a more expensive holiday trip or more time spent on a hobby will produce the satisfied feeling we are after. So this approach results in moving from one relationship to another, from one trip or hobby to another, setting ourselves up to be disappointed because the satisfaction gained from them never remains.

Another wrong approach is simply to *give up on the desires*, to consider them a fantasy, to "move on" to a more realistic activity. Lewis says there is such a man who has given up on his desires. "… He settles down and learns not to expect too much … it would be the best line we could take if man did not live forever."[12] But what a tragedy it would be if infinite happiness were available, and we stopped short of it.

The right way to handle such desires, says Lewis, is to believe that a means of their satisfaction exists. He uses hunger as an example. A child gets hungry; food exists to satisfy that. The challenge comes when we have a desire that "no experience in this world can satisfy."[13] Lewis said, "If I find in myself desires which nothing in this world can satisfy, the only logical explanation is that I was made for another world."[14]

This quote by Lewis serves as a foundation for this book. *There are longings we experience that are present in our heart and mind because we were made for Eden.* If we can reconnect with why God made us, and be reminded how good our purpose really is, we can give thanks for those longings and look forward to their fulfillment.

Lewis' quote also explains why the first two approaches are wrong. One seeks the "right" experience to fulfill a desire that wasn't meant to be fully satisfied on earth. The other tries to negate a desire that God placed there when in fact it is meant to be fulfilled.[15]

Eden and God's Promises

The truth that we are made for another world, one that was without sin in the beginning, and will be again in the end, gives us hope for the hereafter.[16] But what about now, during the days of longing for the fulfillment of those desires? Reminding ourselves of God's promises about what we possess in this life keep the desires alive in us.

Peter says we have everything we need to live as God intended through the power we receive by Jesus living through us.

"Everything we could ever need for life and godliness has already been deposited in us by his divine power. For all this was lavished upon us through the rich experience of knowing him who has called us by name and invited us to come to him through a glorious manifestation of his goodness. As a result of this, he has given you magnificent promises that are beyond all price, so that through the power of these tremendous promises we can experience partnership with the divine nature, by which you have escaped the corrupt desires that are of the world." (2 Peter 1:3-4 TPT)

God displays His goodness so that through the power of His promises we experience partnership with the divine nature that He puts into our spirits. By that power, we can escape the corrupt desires of the world and live for His desires for us! We can live for the right purposes, and long for the right desires, the ones He implants for the return to Eden. We live in a period of history where the effects of sin are on full. We may question the eternal impact of the actions we take as we live the Christ-life. Do they really matter? Can we really do something that contributes to the glory of our

Creator? Yes, we can! We do this by living by magnificent promises of God.

Created with Purpose

This book considers how He redeems us and what He restores to us in the process. Our restoration to God's purpose is a central part of Paul's message. The result of our restoration depends upon a transformation from our sinful selves to a new self, empowered to obey God. That ability is re-established by God's power working through us. The "good news" is only great news if it gives us new power to fulfill our purpose. As we receive His power, God renews our ability to live out His purposes. He has prepared things for us to do by His power. Paul says, "For we are His workmanship, created in Christ Jesus for good works, which God prepared beforehand so that we would walk in them."[17]

How do we live out this purpose? The good works God intends for us to do were already prepared for us before the foundation of the world. He laid out our life's work before we experienced one day on earth.[18] This should give us so much confidence and ease as we walk through difficult days, even days that seem to be producing nothing of eternal value. There are those days we feel we have only "laid up treasure" on earth, not seeing the fingerprint of God on what we attempted or accomplished in that time. But because He made us to be His stewards, He knows those good works He set out for us. They will only be fulfilled and have meaning and impact when we live as He prescribes. *Only when our life is empowered by, and when its worth is measured by, the presence of the life of Jesus working mightily within us, will we fulfill the destiny He placed in us before we took our first breath.*

11

Back to His Original Intent

Being Made for Eden, made in His image and for His purpose in His creation, is an essential component in the "good news" we embrace when we enter God's family. Eden was God's intended reality for mankind. We see this in God's promises and how He describes the life of those He calls as His possession. Jesus' sacrifice on the cross shows us that reconciliation to God, and to His purposes, was God's plan in the incarnation. Colossians 1 says:

> "And by the blood of his cross, everything in heaven and earth is brought back to himself-*back to its original intent, restored to innocence again*! Even though you were once distant from Him, living in the shadows of your evil thoughts and actions, He reconnected you back to Himself. He released his supernatural peace to you through the sacrifice of His own body as the sin-payment on your behalf so that you would dwell in His presence. And now there is nothing between you and Father God, for He sees you as holy, flawless, and restored, if indeed you continue to advance in faith, assured of a firm foundation to grow upon. Never be shaken from the hope of the gospel you have believed in. And this is the glorious news I preach all over the world." (Colossians 1:20 TPT)[19]

The glorious news that Paul proclaimed is that there is nothing between us and the Father now that the reconciliation achieved by the death of a sinless Son of God brings mankind and all creation back to relationship. No sin separates us from Him and His purposes. In His eyes, we are back to being flawless, as mankind was prior to the fall in Eden. We are restored to the original intent!

Restoration is a theme found all throughout the Bible. Restoration to God means restoration to His original intent. When we operate from a right view of God's intended purpose for us, we will understand the high privilege of bearing His likeness. Through our transformation into looking more like Him, God intends to restore us to Eden, to enjoy His presence and His pleasures forever. The restored relationship to God through Jesus fosters our restored purpose. We were "Made for Eden," made in His image, for the purpose of stewarding His creation.

2

Stewards of Eden: What Creation Says About Our Purpose

Being made for Eden means that what Adam and Eve did daily while living in the garden fulfilled a purpose for which God created them. I believe God inspired all the books that became the Bible, and that there is continuity between the Old and New Testaments. Many skeptics like to argue that there is a different portrayal of God in the two Testaments. They believe there exists a God of vengeance in the Old, and a God of love in the New. They consider the Old Covenant to be about rules and punishment, while the New Covenant is about grace and mercy. So what evidence is there to defend the truth that God is the same yesterday, today, and tomorrow, and that His justice, mercy, and grace are all present in God's actions toward mankind across the entire history of the Bible? If He made us for Eden, how does the Bible reflect this unchanging purpose for man? And how does the unity of the Old and New Testaments concerning God's nature reflect that continuing purpose that was established in Eden?

These questions can be answered by a true perspective on God's unchanging nature across the Bible, particularly in how He deals with His people missing the mark He established for them. To conclude that the purpose for man in Eden continues through history to include us means that God was always acting to rescue His people, not judge them for failure. If we see the Old Testament as evidence of God not giving up on His chosen people, but rather sending them deliverers and prophets to continually remind them of His original purpose, then we begin to see several parallels with the New Testament. One, we see Jesus being Messiah as fulfillment of God's promise, for "He will save His people from their sins."[20] Because our forgiveness is the result of a promise of deliverance for God's people through a Messiah, we don't have to be afraid of "messing up," of sinning and pushing God away. Instead, when we do stumble, we repent so that relationship is restored. Two, we can see the compassion and long-suffering of God with Israel as a preview of the traits found in Jesus, who is the exact representation of the Father. Three, we are motivated to be who God meant us to be. We will want to make Him our model for living, as Paul says in Ephesians 5.

Another unified truth between the Testaments is that we are already made in His image; we don't have to *achieve* likeness to Him through good works. Adam and Eve were created in His image. They did not have to achieve likeness. In the New Testament, we are called to do good works, greater works than Jesus did, but we don't do them to earn God's acceptance, pleasure, or salvation. We do them because Jesus already made us acceptable and pleasing to God when we entered the family. When we obey Him in humility, He is pleased. Jesus' baptism is a perfect example. When He allows John to baptize Him, even after John proclaimed himself unworthy to even carry Jesus' sandals, His Father says, "this is my beloved Son, with whom I am well pleased."[21] Jesus saw His baptism as a fulfillment of His Father's will, so He underwent it willingly, humbly.

The goodness of God toward His people is not just a New Testament idea. It was evident in God's revelation to Moses and to David, among others. In Exodus 33, Moses asks God what will distinguish them from all other peoples on earth if God's presence is not with them. God answers that His presence will be with them and He will give them rest. Then Moses asks to see God's glory. God replies that His goodness will pass in front of Moses! His goodness is known to Moses in this moment. And Moses walked around with a glowing face after this encounter.[22]

The same word for goodness appears in Psalm 27:13. There, David encourages his own heart in knowing He will see the goodness of the Lord in the land of the living, meaning on this earth. David had been through many things, even the loss of a child, but was banking on God's goodness in the midst of his pain and loss.

God uses various situations to teach His people Israel why His ways and His commands are really not a burden, but are the path to life. God was patient with His wayward people. Just one instance is when Abraham asks God in Genesis 18 whether He will destroy Sodom if fifty righteous are found within it. God says He will spare the city for the sake of those fifty.

Abraham keeps asking God the same question while lowering the required number. Instead of being irritated with Abraham's persistence, God instead patiently shows His mercy by ultimately rescuing Abraham's family out of the city. When we fit together these pictures of God's mercy and His instruction to His people, we see that the way God relates to Israel is an overflow of His goodness. The requirements about living separate from the peoples around them were to demonstrate holiness, a separateness not meant as restriction for its own sake, but to mark them for serving God's purposes. When we see God using Moses, a killer, and David, an adulterer, making them key figures in Israel's history despite their mistakes, we then appreciate more fully Jesus doing the same with Peter. After Peter denies Jesus three times, we could have never heard from Peter again. But if he believed that Jesus, as the exact representation of God's nature, would condemn him, Peter would never have been the one to preach at Pentecost. He would have never become a key figure in the spread of the message of repentance for the forgiveness of sins. He believed Christ offered forgiveness.[23] In contrast to Peter, Judas remained in his remorse and hanged himself.[24] The choice to believe that God stands ready to overcome our doubt and failure is ours to make. We can hear His voice, calling us to repent and return to Him—to our original "Eden" purpose for which we were created. Both Old and New Testaments attest to the ability for those who are His to hear God. In Isaiah, God says, "and whenever you turn to the right or to the left, your ears will hear this command behind you: 'This is the way. Walk in it.'"[25] Jesus says, "My sheep hear My voice, and I know them, and they follow Me." (John 10:27 NAS 1995)[26]

In various situations in the Old Testament, the mercy and lovingkindness of God is evident. The goodness of God and His desire to use His people for His original purpose is not found only in the New Testament. If we go back to the garden, before the sin of Adam of Eve occurs, to see what God intended in creating mankind, it not only frames our understanding of the events in the Bible, but also establishes the nature of God. His intent for man was not punishment, but real partnership in managing what He created, a noble role intended for all God's children. Each person's way of fulfilling their part of God's purpose will be unique to them. But the call upon each child is to serve Him in His goodness. Within that call, God gifts and shapes each believer so they can embrace their part of stewardship. That specific call is not erased when we fail. Just as God responded to Israel's true repentance, He is pleased and helps us do His will when we get back on the path of obedience. The basis of our relationship is that He first loved us. Nothing can separate us from that love. No amount of idolatry or other disobedience could separate Israel from being the nation through which the redeemer Messiah would come and influence the whole world.

At the core, do we see the same nature of God in both Testaments? When we tie the actions of God back to His original intention of close partnership, and His action to redeem men through Jesus' death and resurrection, then yes. Absolutely, the goodness of God is consistent through the whole Bible. What God was doing in His relationship with all the Old Testament figures, from Noah to Abraham to Moses to David and many others, is showing His mercy to a sinful people. At the right time, He sent His only Son to live a perfect life as a man which made Him the once for all sacrifice to overcome sin and death, and to defeat Satan, a cherub who fell from his place of serving God in heaven through his own rebellion against God.[27] While the natures of the two covenants were different, according to Hebrews 8 and 9, the permanence of God's purpose to love, redeem, and restore is reflected in both Old and New Covenants. In Jesus, our perspective of what God was doing among His people changes. Even in the encounter on the Road to Emmaus, Jesus shows that He is evident in the Old Testament. He says in Luke "'Wasn't it clearly predicted that the Messiah would have to suffer all these things before entering his glory?' Then Jesus took them through the writings of Moses and all the prophets, explaining from all the Scriptures the things concerning Himself." (Luke 24:26-27 NLT)[28] The coming Messiah, and the grace and rescue coming through Him, was evident in all that preceded Jesus' time on earth and the record of what He did and said, and its impact on the Church He was forming was written as our "New Testament."

We need reference points to fully appreciate the message of God's Word, themes to consider as we fit together the many threads of the masterpiece He inspired to further our understanding Him, His ways, and His purpose. I think the truth that we were made for Eden is one of those reference points. To believe this is what we were made for shows us man's life was meant to be in partnership with God! It affirms that God was not a force "out there," who created the universe but then remained separate from it, but that He is present among us. The very name given to Jesus is Emmanuel, which means God with us. God made us for relationship.

In Jesus, this relationship goes even a step further. God is not only with us, He is in us. In John 14, Jesus says:

"If you love Me, you will keep My commands. And I will ask the Father, and He will give you another Counselor to be with you forever. He is the Spirit of truth. The world is unable to receive Him because it doesn't see Him or know Him. But you do know Him, because He remains with you and will be in you. I will not leave you as orphans; I am coming to you. In a little while the world will see Me no longer, but you will see Me. Because I live, you will live too. In that day you will know that I am in My Father, you are in Me, and I am in you. The one who has My commands and keeps them is the one who loves Me. And the one who loves Me will be loved by My Father. I also will love him and will reveal Myself to him ... If anyone loves Me, he will keep My word. My Father will love him, and We will come to him and make Our home with him." (John 14:15-21, 23 HCS)[29]

The Holy Spirit, our counselor, will be with us forever. Not only *with* us, but *in* us according to verse 17. In verse 20, Jesus says He is in us. And verse 23 says the Trinity will make their home with us. Just like God made His presence known to Adam and Eve in Eden, because of the cross, God restored that access to Him by making His presence dwell in us. That is what Jesus said to His disciples as He prepared to leave earth and return to the Father. If we love Him, we will obey Him. He says for us to remain in Him as He does in us. And by remaining, we will bear fruit for Him. Without Him, we can do nothing.

As we explore later in the book what it means to be a new creation, to be sons and daughters, to experience His freedom, to be His messengers, and to overcome this world so that we experience His new heaven and earth, the new Eden, we should have a framework for the story of redemption. Over the course of history, God has shown what He values: people. His current purpose for those He redeems is the same as what He intended in the beginning. He wants a relationship with man through which His excellency is displayed, and His goodness in salvation is made known. It's not about how many times we fail. It is about getting up, repenting, and moving forward in our call as His stewards.

When we do that, our lives matter, for they carry significance, fulfilling the purpose of the One who made us for relationship with Himself. Knowing the reason He made us keeps our life from being about us. He loved us, so we can love Him and love others. Having a fulfilling life is not about meeting the right people, getting the right break in a career path, getting smarter, becoming more attractive, or even being born into privilege.

Because you are already wise. When you receive salvation, you get the mind of Christ. And you are attractive. You carry a light that radiates from your body.[30] Jesus, who is in you, is the radiance of God's glory. Therefore, you are radiant.[31]

And you are "born again" into privilege. You are a child of God Most High. You have an inheritance that can't be taken away. In God's mercy, He birthed you into it. 1 Peter says, "According to His great mercy, He has given us a new birth into a living hope through the resurrection of Jesus Christ from the dead, and into an inheritance that is imperishable, uncorrupted, and unfading, kept in heaven for you." (1 Peter 1:3-4 HCS)[32] You have all you need to live a life of faith before God, He has given His grace freely to you, and out of His riches He provides for you.[33]

So we must avoid focusing on the penalty of death which resulted from sin in Eden. Instead, we must focus on what God began in Eden: a close relationship with the people He called His own. God chose to create Adam and Eve to steward His creation. Later, He birthed the nation of Israel to be His chosen ones as He did with Adam and Eve. He brought Israel out of slavery. He promised them blessing in the land He gave them to settle. In a similar way, He rescued us from our slavery to sin when He bought us back from the enemy's grip. We belong to Him, and He secures our destiny forever.

With the perspective we have living after the events of both testaments, we can trace where the story of God is going. In this book, I want to look at how God expressed His purpose to His chosen ones, so we don't lose heart at the difficulties along the way. Hebrews 11 says that many of God's faithful ones died before receiving the promises, but they saw and believed in them. Stepping back and seeing the unity between the entire story of God and His people stirs our faith and encourages us not to give up before we see final fulfillment of His promises.

Our God-defined Purpose on Earth

To understand the perfect environment we were made to operate in while fulfilling God's purpose, we must go to Genesis. God in three persons, the Trinity, existed first and formed all that was made, including man and his environment. God created mankind with a purpose, distinct from the rest of creation. I believe that purpose has remained consistent across time because the nature of God, and the way He dealt with His people, was consistent. The focus in this chapter is on the impact of God designing mankind's role on earth: to be managers of His creation. How does that role of manager, as steward, prove that we were made for Eden? From Genesis 1:1–2, we conclude some foundational assumptions:

- ➢ One, God is the creator of all.
- ➢ Two, the earth was void until He spoke the elements into existence.
- ➢ Three, He saw that all He created was good.

Mankind's Role in Managing Creation

Genesis 1:26–28 is a description of mankind's creation. Because of its familiarity, we may overlook its significance. God said, "Let Us make man in Our image, according to Our likeness; and let them rule over the fish of the sea and over the birds of the sky and over the cattle and over all the earth, and over every creeping thing that creeps on the earth. God created man in His own image, in the image of God He created him; male and female He created them. God blessed them; and God said to them, Be fruitful and multiply, and fill the earth, and subdue it; and rule over the fish of the sea and over the birds of the sky and over every living thing that moves on the earth."[34]

Mankind was created in the image of God and given responsibilities within the created order. The responsibilities that come with bearing that likeness to God include having a job to do. It is important to see where mankind was placed to perform that job.

"The Lord God <u>planted a garden toward the east, in Eden; and there He placed the man whom He had formed</u>. Out of the ground the LORD <u>God caused to grow</u> every tree that is pleasing to the sight and good for food; the tree of life also in the midst of the garden, and the tree of the knowledge of good and evil. Now a <u>river flowed out of Eden to water the garden;</u>"[35]

"Then the Lord God took the man and put him into the garden of Eden to cultivate it and keep it."[36]

Genesis 1 and 2 show that man and woman were given responsibilities in God's creation. They were:

- ➢ To be fruitful and subdue the earth 1:28
- ➢ To rule (over creation) 1:28
- ➢ To cultivate the garden 2:15

God began a relationship with Adam and Eve that He could not enjoy with the other living things He created. We see this uniqueness and authority established in one of their first tasks: naming the animals. God created the animals, then brought them to Adam for naming. In this, God established mankind's authority over "every beast of the field." By giving the animals names, Adam was in authority over them, as God had purposed in Genesis 1:28.[37]

This is important because what Adam named the animals became their names. God gave Adam the authority to decide that. From the start, God intended for Adam to be a steward of creation, and therefore an enforcer of His purpose. Everything God created was meant to display something about its Creator. There was purpose in every creature He created, but a greater authority was given to man.

What Is a Steward?

A steward is a manager of resources. In the travel industry, a "cabin steward" is someone responsible for the needs of the guest on a cruise ship in staterooms assigned to the steward. He provides personal assistance to guests and aims to create a positive atmosphere for them. He ensures the cleanliness of the staterooms and communicates with customers about things that they need.

In medieval times, an estate steward took care of a Lord's castle while he was away.[38] The steward was a servant who supervised both the lord's estate and his household. In our modern society, a new term in financial management is to call oneself a "wealth steward." One financial firm says, "A growing number of advisors are positioning themselves as Wealth Stewards. The concept of stewardship has often been used in context of the environment, theology, and health. The term at its core means responsible planning and management of resources."[39]

Simply, *a steward is one who wisely plans for the use and management of an owner's resources.* The steward manages resources with the best interest of the owner in mind! That is what God calls us to be: wise managers of all He created and placed under our authority.

Stewards in Scripture

There are many illustrations in the Bible, drawn from human stories, that demonstrate what is expected of a steward or manager. Joseph became a steward in the house of Potiphar in Egypt and had such authority that his master entrusted all his possessions to his care.[40] In the Gospels, the idea of a steward and his master appears often. In the Parable of the Talents, Jesus says a man was going on a journey and turned his possessions over to his servants. In response to the servants who managed those resources wisely, He said, "Well done good and faithful slave ... share your Master's joy!"[41]

Jesus told a parable about a dishonest steward who was called to account for his wasteful ways. He said, "there was a rich man who received an accusation that his manager was squandering his possessions. So he called the manager in and asked, 'What is this I hear about you? Give an account of your management, because you can no longer be my manager'... The master praised the unrighteous manager because he had acted astutely. For the sons of this age are more astute than the sons of light in dealing with their own people. And if you have not been faithful with what belongs to someone else, who will give you what is your own?(HCSB)"[42] The steward is asked to account for his management of the rich man's things. Those who have been entrusted with another's resources are expected to show good results from their management. Jesus also says how we manage what belongs to someone else (God) is a measure of our worthiness to receive things ourselves.

Finally, Paul uses the term "steward" to describe leaders of the Church. He says those who govern the Church should be viewed as God's stewards. In Titus, he says a bishop (overseer) should be blameless as a steward of God.[43] A steward, then, is one who is in charge of and watches over or cares for what is entrusted to him. God made Adam and Eve stewards over all of creation. The New Testament evidence is strong that we are still called to be stewards of His creation. He receives glory from our proper stewardship. As our Master it is His right to evaluate how well we manage the resources He entrusted to us.

My Own Stewardship Journey

Learning about stewardship has taken me many years. We can always grow in our ability to see how God wants us to treat what He has given us. To steward is to watch over, to treat as valuable. As we adopt the view of ourselves as God's stewards, we should consider how we are stewarding our own talents and desires. In my teens, I began to achieve success in school. By the time high school ended, I had been accepted into several colleges of my choice. With my faith clearly a priority, I thought hard about what I wanted in a career. I had a strong sense of wanting to make a difference, to be an influencer for God. I remember sitting at my high school honors night my senior year waiting to hear my name called for scholarships. At night's end, I had received a significant one, given in the name of a beloved educational supporter and business leader in our city. Because of that, I knew people expected me to do important things in my future

I think that academic success helped me tangibly understand this expectation, and the verse which says "for everyone to whom much is given, from him much will be required." (Luke 12:48 NKJV)[44] I didn't feel pressured. But I did feel that God had a career path I didn't want to miss. And it was up to me to find it. I knew how to seek direction from the Bible. But I didn't know how to be guided by the Holy Spirit, as Jesus, in John 16:13, promises will be true for believers after Jesus sends the Spirit. My journey to finding

God's direction for my life wasn't helped as I entered our school building every day. The slogan written there said, "If it's to be, it's up to me." This slogan, while reflecting bits of truth, does not reflect Jesus' full message. The implication is that we are on our own to create positive outcomes in life. And while God does give us a responsibility to act based on what He already promised in His covenant with us, He promises to never leave us. We are not on our own to figure out life. The sense of being "on our own" for success in our purpose has a parallel to the lie in the garden that Satan spoke to Adam and Eve. Satan questioned whether God had really provided all they needed. Or had He withheld the very best from them?

I did not believe God was withholding from me my purpose. But I needed to keep narrowing down the options. To help define what I was made for, I took personality tests and vocational aptitude tests. I did well in college but still searched for what God was shaping me to be passionate about. I thought I wanted to study law and worked in Washington, DC right after graduation. But it was that summer, after a positive but not directionally confirming experience there, that I decided to attend seminary and pursue ministry. I loved the Bible and felt that studying it deeper would show myself "approved unto God as a workman who does not need to be ashamed, accurately handling the word of truth."[45]

Only after a PhD degree, eight years as a pastor, and finally leaving paid ministry to enter into business, did I realize God was less concerned with my job than He was my call. He called me to be His son, to steward things close to His heart, and to help other people know and embrace His true nature. And I could do that in any workplace, any career. Bringing God glory through my life, and the lasting impact of my work is not up to me; it is up to Him *in* me!

We all have to look at His original call to Adam and Eve if we ever hope to honor His design for our unique abilities and passions in serving as His stewards. People turn to other measures in evaluating vocational choices, like where a job is located or how big the salary is. To approach our lives primarily based on how we earn money to support ourselves is to miss the bigger picture of why mankind is on earth in the first place. If we want to connect to His purpose that began at creation, we must be sure we are not measuring our purpose by the world's ideas, but rather by who God says we are.

New Testament Fulfillment of Created Purpose: We Are His Workmanship, Kings and Priests

Ephesians 2:10 shows that we are God's creation, and the deeds He set out for us to do were prepared beforehand for us.[46] As the animals were created before mankind, preparing the way for Adam to fulfill God's design to rule over creation, so God goes before believers to fulfill the works He ordains for them. But that preparation must start by us believing we were "made for Eden" and embracing the stewardship role we received in Eden. Then we must believe that our original role as stewards over creation was not destroyed by Adam's or our own sin. Sin made Adam's role harder (there will be toil in working the ground), but did not change God's purpose for him or the rest of mankind.[47] We, like Adam, must steward what He, our Master, prepares for us.

Under the new covenant, we see another aspect of our stewardship over creation. John says, as His kings and priests, we are to rule and reign on the earth. "And they sang a new song, saying, 'Worthy are You to take the scroll and to break its seals; for You were slaughtered, and purchased people for God with Your blood from every tribe, language, people and nation. You have made them into a kingdom and priests to our God; and they will reign upon the earth.'"[48] We are designed to serve God with holy lives as priests, and to rule over the new earth.[49] The Master bought us, and He is worthy of our service. He invites us to rule and reign.

The common element between these identities of stewards, kings, and priests is that mankind gets back the authority he forfeited in the fall in Eden. We once again are instruments of God's purpose on earth when we rule by His authority. Jesus came to destroy the works of Satan, to reverse the curse sin placed on us, and to restore us as stewards.

Evidence We Were Made for Eden: Creation Groans for Stewards

At creation, mankind was made to steward the rest of God's creation. The New Testament affirms this role. What does God say about the state of creation as it awaits complete renewal? And how are we to view what God has created? I believe the view God intended us to have of creation is still present inside us. I will illustrate, and then turn to Paul for his answer.

Several years ago there were some changes in my family's life that made me realize how much our hearts are wired for Eden. First, several members of our family purchased farm acreage and began growing vegetables and fruits there. We talked about the reasons for the move, then, fairly quickly, found the right location. It took almost two years of clearing woods, seeding grass, and building a road before we finally began building the house we would call home.

As much as I love the outdoors, and always have, I had forgotten what the solitude and "country quiet" can do for our sense of rest and peace. Many nights I watch the sun set over the ridge we face from our porch, observing the moment-by-moment change of the sky's color as it marks the close of another day. Creation doing what God wrote into its design to do.

The feeling I get when I drive onto the property is one of connection to my Father. The earth is indeed our Father's world. The experiences of watching our garden grow, then harvesting it and eating what it produces, also remind me of the cycle of seasons God instituted. Being closer to nature has made me appreciate what the world may call small pleasures. Things like hearing a flowing stream after a good rain, or watching deer and turkey roam the property. Or appreciating seeing these animals with their young which reminds me of the nurture God demonstrates through mothers and fathers, both natural and spiritual.

In short, living close to the land gives me a picture of God walking with Adam and Eve in Eden. He created a beautiful environment for them to live in, where they were connected, not only with that environment where their needs were provided, but also with God in the light of His presence. We know He was present in that garden because Genesis 3:8 says Adam and Eve heard the sound of God walking in the cool of the day. And He asks Adam where they are. Adam says when they heard God there they hid themselves. God asks where they are not because He can't locate them, but to get them to admit why they hid. In His omniscience, He knew what they had done and where they were. God's question drew from Adam the reply, "I was afraid because I was naked, so I hid." (Genesis 3:10, HCS)[50] We were meant to dwell in His constant presence. But sin placed a barrier between us and God that made that impossible unless God intervened. God did have a plan to remove that barrier, and He accomplished it in Jesus on the cross. But after their disobedience, stewardship immediately became more difficult than it was before sin entered the world.

I believe one of the reasons we have difficulty recognizing how being made for Eden should shape our life on earth is this: the vast majority of human history takes place after sin entered God's perfect creation. *Thus our sample of the Eden life is small.* But God's decision to create mankind, place them in the garden, and give them dominion over creation clearly demonstrates His intention. And it sets up the reason for the restoration of all things, including a new heaven and new earth.[51] When Satan has received his final judgment as Revelation 20 describes, we will physically return to the existence we were always meant for. The dwelling place of God will be among men, as it was in Eden.

In light of our clear call to be stewards of creation, Paul says creation is waiting for redemption, waiting on God's children to awaken to their role as stewards. In Romans 8:19-22 he says:

"For the anxious longing of the creation waits eagerly for the revealing of the sons of God. For the creation was subjected to futility, not willingly, but because of Him who subjected it, in hope that the creation itself also will be set free from its slavery to corruption into the freedom of the glory of the children of God. For we know that the whole creation groans and suffers the pains of childbirth together until now." (NAS 1995)[52]

What exactly is the freedom of the glory of the children of God? And what do creation's suffering and "groans" describe? Creation suffering the pains of childbirth refers back to the curse spoken to Eve in the garden, the consequence of her sin. The process of childbirth would be painful, as a reminder of the disobedience to God. In a figurative way, creation also experiences the pangs, the "groans" of being affected by the fall of men. Creation is waiting for the Sons of God (men and women) who know the inheritance we were made for to return to their role as stewards. Men and women who take earthly stewardship seriously, not leaving the task of watching over the earth to radical people who are pushing agendas. It is freedom from corruption, from all of creation being dimmed in the expression of its glory by the presence of sin. True freedom is the state of reflecting the glory we, and all of creation, were meant to display from the beginning.

Why should we not believe that the God who redeemed us, who ordained our good works to bring Him glory, would also redeem our environment? It is on this majestic earth that we were to return to Him the love He first loved us with. Because God appointed us as its stewards, our efforts at redeeming the earth are worth it. We are restored to our purpose by which we reign with Him in heaven, but also in order to be stewards of the restored earth. The answer to the question of what Paul viewed as the destiny for followers of Jesus may surprise you, given modern thinking in the Church is that "going to heaven" is the realm where we experience the fulfillment of our longings, and where God fulfills His promise to be with and among us. If we accept our role as earthly stewards, we join creation's groanings for redemption as it waits for freedom from its imperfections.

Stewarding Earth as His Gift

Lest we think of stewardship as a burden or an obligation, let's look again at Genesis 1. At original creation, the Trinity said, "let us make man in our image, after our likeness. And let them have dominion." (Genesis 1:26 ESV)[53] God doesn't just *make* mankind have authority over living things, He *lets* them have it. If we want to fully experience God's purpose for us, we must accept that role of dominion over creation and live it out. But before we will engage in the privilege of doing what we were meant to do, we need to understand that we are "Made for Eden"—made to rule over His earth. In doing what we were meant to do, we fulfill who we were meant to be. The potter knows how he made the clay and knows the best "shape" it should take to fulfill the desire of the maker. God made mankind to fulfill a role, to exercise a dominion that mankind alone can fulfill. Animals cannot fulfill our purpose, neither can angels.

God designed us to be awed by the nature we see around us. He made it for us to enjoy, as a reminder of a creative God. He placed a creative imprint of His presence on the earth through what He made. Paul says in Romans 1:20 that God is clearly seen in what He creates.[54] God made his creation a witness on the earth to the Eden we were made for. It is a witness not only to a beautiful creation, but to the Creator Who wanted us to experience some of the majesty that will be ours in the future Eden.

But we are not at that place in the story now. Before we can understand the richness of that destiny, we must consider why Adam and Eve were banished from the first Eden, as well as the extreme action God took to provide us a future Eden. It's time to wake up to our role as stewards and work at it with diligence. But effectiveness in this role requires a correct view of our Master, and of how God treats those who serve Him. Our stewardship is hindered when we have an incorrect view of God's character.

3

Separation from Eden (and Why We Don't Realize Eden Is Still Ours)

To know what incredible lengths God went to to re-establish our place in His story and plans, we have to see how far sin took Adam and Eve—and therefore us—from Him. Their sin in Eden separated them from the blessings flowing from a partnership with God. Their actions in Eden began a long history of mankind choosing sin over the inheritance God promised. In order to fully understand the effects of their sin, let's look at history.

A Survey of History: Sinners and Saints

The previous chapter demonstrated that God will restore to His sons and daughters what He intended for them to enjoy from the very beginning of creation. If we really understood the offer in that, we would be the most joyful creatures on earth. Because without His grace, we would be excluded from the life of God.[55] But experiencing sufficient joy over God's offer of restoration requires us to understand the extent of the effects of sin.

In the garden, the blessing of living in God's presence was interrupted by sin, and once sin entered mankind's consciousness, its fruit was evident. Genesis records that it did not take long for murder to occur (Cain and Abel), for false views in relating to God to surface (Tower of Babel), and for treachery to invade (Joseph's brothers selling him into slavery).

Despite their sin, there were Israelites who enjoyed the blessing of God's presence with them. Consider Moses' place in Israel's history. He experiences God's glory while on Mount Sinai for forty days, receiving the Ten Commandments. And in answer to Moses' request to see God's glory, God agrees to have His goodness pass by the rock where Moses is standing. But Moses cannot see God's face and live, so he sees only His back.[56] Seeing even God's back, and the power of His goodness passing by, was enough to produce a visible effect on Moses. Exodus says that after Moses talked with God on Sinai, his face shone just from the exposure to God's glory.[57] When Moses entered the tent of meeting, where God would speak to him, he describes that communication as "face to face, just as a man speaks to his friend.(HCSB)"[58]

Yet while Moses was on Sinai, the Israelites formed a god out of gold to worship, violating God's command to worship Him only. So despite Moses' obedience to God, the nation he led constantly fell short of God's plans, following their sin nature rather than their Creator. God eventually sent His prophets and judges to both show Israel how they fell short, and to entreat them to return to Him. After a long period, He then sent His Son. Paul was inspired to say "when the fullness of time came, God sent His Son" to redeem those under Law.[59] All throughout history, from Israel's early days until the Messiah came, man's actions have demonstrated that the sin first present in Eden still needed a remedy.

The World Jesus Entered

As ancient history continued, new empires arose, while sin maintained its hold. Rome became the greatest empire the world had known. Jesus was born under the reign of this Roman Empire, whose thirst for blood was well-established by their practices of gladiator fights and chariot races to the death throughout the empire. They focused on conquest, submission of people groups and enslavement of those in their path, abusing the power they held. Jesus chose the role of a suffering servant, doing the Father's will, to redeem men and restore the close fellowship of men and God. To choose serving over ruling was just as unusual a position then, in the context of Roman rule, as it is today. Yet Jesus modeled love for all people without regard to their position, and He chose to serve people rather than rule over them.

This survey of history shows that from the early persecution of "The Way" under Nero, to the establishment of the Christian faith under Constantine, to the practice of indulgences in the Middle Ages, to the humanism of the Renaissance, religious authorities set expectations for how faith should be exercised. The expression of one's own faith in God always faced these religious constraints, which sought to define how one should relate to God. Yet often those who exerted this influence did not reflect the example of Jesus. In the days of Jesus, position and power were obtained, not by inheritance from emperor to next emperor, but by treachery and violence. The centuries to follow would hold just as much bloodshed in the pursuit of power and authority. Jesus came in the opposite spirit. Rather than trying to control others from a position of authority, He laid His life down for humanity. He left His place of power and authority in heaven as the supreme being and suffered as a man in order to free mankind from the systems that oppressed them. The struggle for position and power wasn't reserved for politics. There were several groups Jesus encountered who were each trying to exert their influence. Pharisees, Sadducees, Gnostics, and others all felt they had a corner on truth. But Jesus came to give His life and show that only He was the gateway to the Father. He defined what makes a life pleasing and useful to God. Man's ideas of what makes a person qualified to fulfill God's holy purpose made it harder for even the truly devout seeker of truth to grasp God's plan.

"Holy Ones" of God Are Saints

Religions that have arisen after Jesus' time on earth have tried to tangibly express how individuals should pursue a relationship with God. Man's ideas about the path to holiness in God's eyes can lead seekers away from the biblical truth. In the quest to lead people closer to God, the focus can shift to outward piety. Who can design the bigger and more elaborate houses of worship to reflect and magnify the value of God? And which "important" people distinguished themselves in service to others and to God, and in high esteem, are given titles like "bishop," "prophet," or "saint"? Monuments, cathedrals, and chapels are built in their honor.

But God views the contribution of people to His kingdom differently than the world does. He says His thoughts are not our thoughts.[60] He intentionally uses weak things to confound the wise.[61] God demonstrates this through many people, but just two examples are the choice of David among this brothers as the future king, and of Moses to be Israel's deliverer from Pharoah.[62] Because God alone knows what is in the heart of man, and determines our usefulness to His purposes, His view of sainthood is the important one, not religion's. Paul understands this and calls *all those who are*

38

loved by God, and who are *set apart in Jesus,* "saints." They are, by their identification with Jesus, "called" or marked by God as saints. It is not a description of their worthiness, but rather of their acceptance by God and readiness to serve Him. God calls us saints once we are redeemed by the death and resurrection of Jesus. Those who are called saints by God are qualified for this identity by Jesus' sacrifice which reconciles men to God and sets them apart as God's own.[63] The sufficiency of that sacrifice means God can declare us His holy ones.

Why does defining who God calls "holy" matter to our study of Eden? Because just as God marked Adam and Eve as His stewards of the garden, so He calls all disciples of Jesus to be His holy people, set apart for His purpose. It's not man's job to designate who God values in the work of His kingdom. If anything, God says those He honors as examples of faith and obedience will usually be viewed in the opposite way by man.

> "But God chose those whom the world considers foolish to shame those who think they are wise, and God chose the puny and powerless to shame the high and mighty. He chose the lowly, the laughable in the world's eyes— nobodies—so that he would shame the somebodies. For he chose what is regarded as insignificant in order to supersede what is regarded as prominent, so that there would be no place for prideful boasting in God's presence. *For it is not from man that we draw our life* but from God as we are being joined to Jesus, the Anointed One.(TPT)"[64]

So those people whom the world views as insignificant may well be most honored in God's eyes. A saint is not saintly by virtue of man's designation, but by God calling him "child."

I grew up in a religious tradition where personal morality was a significant measure of one's Christian maturity. The more I did the right things, and avoided the wrong things, the more pleasing I would appear in God's sight. The message was "make sure your good outweighs your bad." While subtle, giving that message any credence was a hindrance to my relationship with God because the truth is He sees me as a saint, set apart for Him. The works-based view of right and wrong implies only a servant-master relationship, i.e., "do as God says and things will go well for you." Yet Jesus tells His disciples in John 15 that we are not just servants, but friends, for we know what His Father, the Master, is doing.

The same perspective on morality and maturity that I encountered, that limits the measure of our faith to simply doing more good than bad, also views the commands of God narrowly. They are seen as absolutes. In effect, "you must not fail to do these if you want to please God." And of course, these commands were more than just suggestions for Israel to follow. But the word for command is better viewed as precept or principle. Do them, and you will operate by His blessing, by how life was meant to work in God's design in Eden. In John 5, Jesus shows that life is found not in a command but in a person.[65] There Jesus says we can miss Him, the Author of life, by focusing only on knowing the Bible's content. He, not the record of His words, is the giver of life. Following principles or commands has value, but real fruit results from intimacy with the Lifegiver. We must come to God as One who rewards those who seek Him, not as One waiting to punish us if we sin against His.

Those who know without doubt that we were made for Eden, and that we are enabled to serve His purpose by Jesus taking the penalty of our sin, will act knowing that God calls us saints. Because He means for us to live "set apart" lives, we will serve Him in light of our position: made holy in His eyes.

But even for those who know what we were made for, there is more to living by His purposes.

Seeing Ourselves as Saints, Serving a Loving God

As we make sense of the effects of Adam and Eve's sin and removal from Eden, there are two understandings. These understandings are intimately tied, and each necessary, for us today who know we are made for Eden. To embrace being set apart by God as stewards, we must have a right understanding of ourselves, and a right understanding of God who made us. *We will see that the sin in Eden was due to the lack of a right understanding of either.* There are serious consequences of a false view of God's nature, and therefore a false view of our *own place* in His creation. When we have a false view of His nature, we miss out on opportunities for blessings, both now and at His return. What type of view of Him would keep us from that close relationship? A view of God that mistrusts His goodness to His highest creation: mankind.

Possible False Views of God and Their Results

A big hindrance to believing we were made for Eden is misunderstanding the nature of God. To see Him as a punisher who shuns and separates Himself from us distorts our view of how He wants our lives to function. In earthly relationships, those who feel they disappoint their parents, or are made to feel unworthy for not doing or saying the right thing, are not interested in hearing the plans their parents put forward. We live in a society in which many of us shun those who punish or disregard us. It is easy to do the same with God if we mistrust His intentions. Fearing God instead of having holy awe for Him leads to a loss of understanding of what He intends for us, or a lack of motivation to follow that intention.

In other words, even if a study of Scripture convinces someone that they are made for Eden and are empowered to live life in light of that truth, their view of God can prevent them from actually *wanting* that life, or being motivated to deny themselves to follow Jesus. The pursuit of a life made into a new creation by Jesus, in-dwelt by His Spirit, and glorifying the Father, depends on the individual's beliefs about God's nature.

When we mistrust His nature, we are afraid of His reaction to anything we do contrary to His expectation. Then as a result, we try to control situations and outcomes. The sin in the garden was the first instance of this cycle of fear and control. As a result, a Redeemer, God himself in the flesh, is called to our rescue. But to see the depth of mankind's sin situation, we must go back to the fall that occurred in Eden.

Where a Wrong View of God Takes Us

God made Eden as the setting for mankind to fulfill His purpose. Genesis 2 makes this clear. Man was created outside the garden, and then brought into it. God formed this garden, and in it he placed Adam and Eve.

> "The LORD God planted a garden toward the east, in Eden; and there He placed the man whom He had formed. Out of the ground the LORD God caused to grow every tree that is pleasing to the sight and good for food; the tree of life was also in the midst of the garden, and the tree of the knowledge of good and evil."[66]

Man had open access to trees that were both good for food and pleasing to the eye. Then we see the command God gave them.

> "Then the LORD God took the man and put him into the Garden of Eden to cultivate it and tend it. The LORD God commanded the man, saying, "From any tree of the garden you may eat freely; but from the tree of the knowledge of good and evil you shall not eat, for in the day that you eat from it you will surely die."[67]

They were free to eat from the tree of life—actually from any tree but the tree of the knowledge of good and evil. Their obedience to this command was a test of their view of God. That test came courtesy of the serpent, the fallen angel, Satan.

"Has God indeed said, 'You shall not eat of every tree of the garden'?" And the woman said to the serpent, 'We may eat the fruit of the trees of the garden; but of the fruit of the tree which *is* in the midst of the garden, God has said, 'You shall not eat it, nor shall you touch it, lest you die.'" Then the serpent said to the woman, "You will not surely die. For God knows that in the day you eat of it your eyes will be opened, and you will be like God, knowing good and evil.(NKJV)"[68]

Adam and Eve sinned by believing they needed *to do something* to be like God. The truth is that they were already like God.[69] We are not the same as God; He has qualities—such as omniscience—that we do not. But when He created us, He stamped us as His own, giving us His likeness. According to Scripture, mankind is the only creation that bears this likeness.

Satan, in tempting Eve, casts doubt on the accuracy and truthfulness of God's Word, then contradicts that Word by claiming to know more than God did about their lives. Ultimately, the consequence of their choice to eat the fruit was their removal from "the garden in Eden." They were also no longer permitted to eat from the tree of life.

> "Then the LORD God said, 'Behold, the man has become like one of Us, knowing good and evil; and now, he might stretch out his hand, and take also from the tree of life, and eat, and live forever'- therefore the LORD God sent him out from the garden of Eden, to cultivate the ground from which he was taken. He drove the man out; and at the east of the garden of Eden He stationed the cherubim and the flaming sword which turned every direction to guard the way to the tree of life.(NAS 1995)"[70]

Mankind was driven out of Eden because God did not want them under the penalty of sin for eternity. God had intended for Adam and Eve to obey His commands—specifically, to eat any of the fruit except the fruit from the tree of knowledge. The decision God made in response to their sin was to remove them from the garden. Otherwise, they would again eat the fruit of the tree of life. If they had done this, they would have lived forever in a fallen state, under the curse of their sin. Genesis 3:24 says God assigned cherubim to guard the entrance to the garden. Adam and Eve were made for the garden but would not experience the fullness of that life God created them for as long as sin separated them from Him.

In Genesis 3, we see that after they sinned, they felt shame, and tried to control the situation by sewing fig leaves to cover themselves. Then Adam blamed Eve for giving him the fruit, and she, in turn, blamed the serpent, Satan.[71]

To emphasize how important it is to God that we see His character rightly, Jesus explains **that His hearers had the same type of fear that Adam and Eve had.** As fear of the Master hindered the decision Adam and Eve made when they believed the deceiver, so it hinders those who serve Him today.

Fear of the Master: The Root Issue Separating God and Man

Fear of the Master comes from a wrong view of God. In the Parable of the Talents, Jesus highlights a parallel with the sin in the Garden of Eden. In this parable, the evil servant says he was afraid, so he hid his talents. Jesus was telling us that using what gifts God graciously grants us *requires seeing Him for who He is*, not viewing Him as demanding more than is reasonable. In Matthew 25, Jesus says

> "And the one also who had received the one talent came up and said, 'Master, I knew you to be a hard man, reaping where you did not sow and gathering where you scattered no *seed*. And I was afraid, and went away and hid your talent in the ground. See, you have what is yours.' But his master answered and said to him, 'You wicked, lazy slave, you knew that I reap where I did not sow and gather where I scattered no *seed*. Then you ought to have put my money in the bank, and on my arrival I would have received my *money* back with interest.(NAS 1995)"[72]

The reply of the master is basically that his servant should have acted based on his perception of the master. If the servant felt the master reaped where he did not sow, he should have at least protected what the master gave him. If he had produced *something* beyond the amount he was given, he would have been prepared for the master to reap beyond the sowing. The evil servant failed to act based on his expectation of his Master. He was afraid and hid his talent in the ground. His attempt to control the outcome is evident in his reply: you have what is yours. In effect, that servant limited the outcome of the situation to one in which no loss could occur. He intended to preserve the gift and give the Master back exactly what he was given.

The parallels with Genesis are very similar.

Genesis 3:5–10	Matthew 25:24–27
View of God	**View of God**
God is a withholder of good things	God takes good things from the sower reaping (the tree was good food, wisdom, a delight to the eyes) where you did not sow
Fear	**Fear**
I heard you, was afraid, and hid myself	I was afraid, and went away and hid your talent in the ground
Consequence	**Consequence**
Because you ate of the tree I commanded you not to, cursed is the ground, in toil you will eat of it	Take away his talent and give it to another - throw out the worthless slave
Control	**Control**
Cover themselves. Blame others.	Respond "You have what is yours." (justify own inaction)

The comparison of these accounts demonstrates that fear of God (fear of the Master) was foremost a result of not understanding God's character and what He has said about

His plans for mankind. Those who follow Jesus face the same choice Adam and Eve did on how to view God. Is the Master a hard man, or is He the Creator who made His highest creation in His image so they could carry out His will on earth? Is He an unjust evaluator of His servants' activities, or a giving Master who wishes them to benefit by multiplying the gift, and therefore be called good and faithful servants?

The reasons Adam and Eve lost access to what God meant for them are very similar to the point behind Jesus' parable. *When fear of the Master/Creator is allowed to take root, it keeps us from fulfilling His purposes.* In short, we miss out on our inheritance when we fear the Giver of that gift and shrink back from doing what He calls us to do because we doubt His goodness and fairness. But even though Adam and Eve forfeited what was theirs, the inheritance God has for all His redeemed children remains a reality. So why do we not realize it is ours to possess?

Why We Don't Realize Eden is Still Our Inheritance

There are several reasons man has not grasped that Eden—the place created without sin present—will again be ours.

- ➤ Paul says unless we understand the redemption that Jesus brings to a believer, we fail to grasp the meaning of the old covenant.
- ➤ The enemy, Satan, blinds the eyes of the unbeliever to truth, especially regarding the goodness of God and the greater promise of the New Covenant.
- ➤ The ruler of this world is active until the time of his final judgment.

Let's consider these in detail from Paul's letters. 2 Corinthians 3 and 4 help us see God's goodness and the promise of the

New Covenant that God is still at work through men to accomplish His purposes. There Paul says:

> "Therefore having such a hope, we use great boldness in *our* speech, and *are* not like Moses, *who* used to put a veil over his face so that the sons of Israel would not look intently at the end of what was fading away. But their minds were hardened; for until this very day at the reading of the old covenant the same veil remains unlifted, because it is removed in Christ. But to this day whenever Moses is read, a veil lies over their heart; but whenever a person turns to the Lord, the veil is taken away.(NAS 1995)"[73]

When we turn to the Lord, the veil is taken away! We are filled with His Spirit and are then able to benefit from the ministry of the Spirit to convict and to counsel us. Operating under the new covenant and the Spirit's power brings clarity to the promises in Jesus, and to what God was doing to demonstrate redemption of His people in the old covenant. But Satan, through deception, reinforces the effect of the veil on those who fail to see the perfection of God's plan for redemption that the new covenant represents. As he did in the garden, he blinds the eyes of those who might understand the truth and be changed by it. Paul says, "And even if our gospel is veiled, it is veiled to those who are perishing, in whose case the god of this world has blinded the minds of the unbelieving so that they might not see the light of the gospel of the glory of Christ, who is the image of God. (NAS 1995)"[74] The "light" or truth of the gospel is that Jesus is the image of His Father, and represents His nature.

Our job is to tear down the lying thoughts that Satan uses to cast doubt on the character and intention of God. Satan's strategy with Eve was to plant thoughts that cast doubt on the

Father's words. As we saw in the parallels with the parable in Matthew, fear and control are the enemy's tools.

Paul says we play an active role in keeping the enemy from building a fortress of lies in our mind about God. To keep Satan from building the walls higher and higher, we must see that the battle for supremacy in our minds is just that: a war. But our weapons are divinely powerful. God is the victor over Satan in the war to keep us from knowing the truth about our inheritance. Paul says in 2 Corinthians 10:4-5 "for the weapons of our warfare are not of the flesh, but divinely powerful for the destruction of fortresses. *We are* destroying speculations and every lofty thing raised up against the knowledge of God, and *we are* taking every thought captive to the obedience of Christ." (NAS1995)[75]

To rightly see the truth about being made for Eden, and about the God who made us for it, we must "take captive" any ideas the enemy brings to suggest we have lost our right to be God's instruments on earth. To be restored to the original blessing Adam received—partnership with God on the earth—requires reconciliation with God. Reconciliation is based on a right view of God and His purpose for our lives, which sets us free to live in relationship with Him and fulfill that purpose.

The Blessing of a Right View of God, and Results of the Sacrifice of Jesus

A right view of God requires seeing that the original blessing God gave to mankind can be restored. That restoration comes through what Jesus' sinless life does for us. He lived the obedient life that pleased His Father, and by this, was able to restore the gift of Eden life to all who are "in Him." When God redeemed us from the death penalty of sin, we changed kingdoms, from "the domain of darkness," to the kingdom belonging to and ruled by Jesus.[76] Now, because God bought us back, we can enter the new heaven and earth He intended for us. He broke down the dividing wall between Israel and the gentiles, so that both receive benefit from God's covenants.

Paul says "Therefore remember that formerly you ... strangers to the covenants of promise, having no hope and without God in the world. But now in Christ Jesus you who formerly were far off have been brought near by the blood of Christ. For He Himself is our peace, who made both *groups into* one and broke down the barrier of the dividing wall ... so that in Himself He might make the two into one new man, *thus* establishing peace ..."[77]

Like the story in Luke 15 of the son who was far off and was brought near by His Father, we who were far off have now been brought near by the blood of Christ. We are reconciled to God!!

What Is Lost When We Have a Wrong View of God

What Adam lost by his shame and fear was the unhindered path to fulfilling his stewardship of the earth. Because of sin, it became harder to glean from our efforts as stewards what we need for our existence.[78] Adam and Eve's choice also produced a condition of the heart, an inclination toward sin, among their descendants, and that inclination grieved God. Genesis 6:5-9 says:

"Then the LORD saw that the wickedness of man was great on the earth, and that every intent of the thoughts of his heart was only evil continually. The LORD was sorry that He had made man on the earth, and He was grieved in His heart. The LORD said, "I will blot out man whom I have created from the face of the land, from man to animals to creeping things and to birds of the sky; for I am sorry that I have made them." But Noah found favor in the eyes of the LORD. These are *the records of* the generations of Noah. Noah was a righteous man, blameless in his time; Noah walked with God." (NAS 1995)[79]

Noah was a picture of the man God had wanted from the beginning. He walked with God, as God intended for Adam and Eve in Eden. Because of this, God spared him and his family from the judgment of the flood. And throughout Israel's history, there were godly and godless leaders, both righteous and unrighteous in their actions. But through those generations, God was repeating His promise, through his prophets, of a Redeemer from the line of David who would rescue God's people. This is why the fulfillment of the promise of the Messiah was hoped for so expectantly. According to Matthew 1:21, there was coming a Son who would be named Jesus, for He will save His people from their sins.

So God has, ever since the rebellion in Eden, been working to fulfill His plan to redeem for Himself a people, from every tribe, tongue, people, and nation.[80] Jesus was considered slain before the foundation of the world.[81] The Father had a provision for erasing the penalty of sin before there was even a problem of a human sin. His desire for a people who will not only rule over earth, but also its peoples, as kings and priests, was never in jeopardy.[82] He accomplishes what He plans. Therefore, the effects of mankind's rebellion were not permanent; they did not tie God's hands. He made a covenant with His people that He will fulfill. In order to fulfill it, He makes us new. We are born again as new creations.

4

The Return to Eden Through Becoming New Creations in Christ

We saw in the last chapter that although Adam and Eve's sin separated them from the life they were meant for, that life is still available for us to experience. So if the life we were meant for is still ours to claim, how do we get it back? To regain the life God intended for us and fulfill His purpose—to experience a return to Eden—we must become new people.

Returning to the Life God Intended

The first foundational truth for returning to the life God intended is that we must lose our own life. A return to the kind of life God offered in Eden requires setting aside any idea that our lives are our own. Jesus says, "he who has lost his life for my sake will find it." (Matthew 10:39 NAS1995)[83] In other words, life, whether filled with joy or sorrow, pleasure or pain, is not about us. Despite the sinful rebellion in the garden, God was continually at work, being faithful to His promise of restoration. The life God intended is infused with His presence and power. We serve Him as master, but know Him as Father, and know Jesus as Savior and friend. Obeying Him does not mean *doing more* in order to make God accept us, like us, or use us for His purposes. Unfortunately, religion conditions people to meet stated or unstated expectations in order to be loved by God or to feel useful to the kingdom of God.

To lose our life for His sake, in order to live as we were meant to—as Adam and Eve experienced before their sin—requires an intentional turn away from sin and the world. Our flesh naturally leans toward sin. The world's influence, alongside the efforts of our enemy to entangle us, together strengthen sin's hold on our flesh. When give in to the temptation to sin, it hinders our pursuit of what we were truly made for, because sin separates us from Him. The answer to overcoming sin is not to deny all desire. Rather, the answer is in fulfilling our desires the way God designed. *It's going to require turning away from the world and its ways, and turning toward God, to get back the life we were built for.* We must start with knowing that we are called to be like Him, in whose image we were created.

The Command: Be Imitators of God

The lie that Satan tried to convince Eve to believe was that she had to do something to be like God. But God had already made her in His image. Paul takes this truth and draws a conclusion: if we were made like Him, then we should look like Him.

But how can we look like Him? By being *transformed* into creatures who can relate to God like Adam and Eve did before the Fall. Jesus calls it being *born again*. Paul says we become new creations. Both describe the same reality: God makes us able to follow Him without the weight of our sin holding us back. The goal of becoming new creations is demonstrating God's qualities like Adam and Eve were created to in the garden. Paul says the life of a disciple involves being imitators of God, as beloved children.[84] The people God has called to Himself and equipped for His purposes are called to be *like Him*.[85] In Acts, we see that early believers were first called Christians at Antioch, literally meaning "little Christs."[86] They acted like the one they were following, so much so that others noticed and described them this way. And according to Acts 4:13, when Peter proclaimed it was by the name of Jesus that a man brought before him was healed, they observed his and John's boldness. When the observers discerned, based on their education, how "unprepared" Peter and John were to offer such a bold message, their conclusion was amazement. And they recognized that they had been with Jesus. These disciples got their boldness from the Bold One, Jesus. Throughout His ministry, as He taught and healed and spent time with His closest followers, Jesus was literally modeling for them what living close to the Father's heart and will looks like. He also wanted to be an example of the resulting intimate relationship, authority, and power available to those who have faith in their Father.

Jesus was so committed to His Father's will that He only did what He saw His Father doing. Doing our Father's will should be our aim also. Yet our culture sends the "not so subtle" message instead, that if our life just imitated those of exemplary people in athletics, business, and entertainment, we would, at the end of our days, have done something with our life. Paul says we should desire to be little Christs, to strive to imitate, and thus reflect the likeness to our heavenly Father that comes with being made in His image. Jesus clearly wasn't looking to imitate others on earth—only His Father. We too are to be imitators of God, not imitators of men.

Certainly, there are godly traits in others worth imitating. But Paul says our admiration should rest on the proper person. When Paul commanded a man at Lystra, who had been lame since birth, to stand up, the crowd believed the gods had come to earth in the form of man. They even began calling Paul "Hermes" and Barnabas "Zeus," the identities of Greek gods. In anguish that the people were putting them on par with a god, Paul and Barnabas tore their robes in disgust. Paul declared "we are men also, with the same nature as you, and we are proclaiming good news to you." (Acts 14:12-18, HCS)[87] In other words, we are just messengers, sent to call you out from serving worthless idols to serve the living God.[88]

Our focus cannot be on human actions, human goodness, or earthly power. Paul's perspective is that we are only messengers, and the focus is not on our goodness or our power. So how can our lives be restored to our created purpose, to truly act like "little Christs"? This is only possible when Jesus turns us into reflections of Himself. Paul says that Christ is being "formed in us," and lives His life in us and through us. To live the life God meant us for, we must become a new creation which enables us to fulfill the command to imitate Him. I find that the writing of C.S. Lewis explains well what being a "new creation" is.

The Fulfillment: Being New Creations, Little Christs

In his timeless book, *Mere Christianity*, in the essay "Is Christianity Hard or Easy," Lewis speaks of us becoming new creatures once our old self dies. God creates the new man, and Christ comes to live His life in us. Once Jesus comes to us, God looks at us as existing "in Christ." By bringing the life of Jesus into our own, the Father sees the likeness in us we were meant to have. We *allow the life of Jesus to be lived through us, as a beloved child of God.* Jesus living His life through us is the key for us to return to the purpose we are made for. [89]

Why is "putting on Jesus" so essential? It is vital because *life in the presence of God in the Garden of Eden depended on obedience, and we need the benefit of Jesus' obedience to be able to return to that life.* The only way we can receive the promise of returning to Eden is by putting on Christ. Humbling ourselves and acknowledging that He is the way to the Father means seeing that our lives can only fulfill their purpose in Him. When we acknowledge this, we welcome the power and presence of Jesus into our relationships, our thinking, and our decisions. The life of Jesus in us is our hope for experiencing life as a child of God, as it was meant to be in Eden. *He makes us new so that we are able to imitate Him and experience the life we were meant for.*

Having a child is one of the most joyous gifts on earth. It surely has been for me. Part of what we love about babies is their growing understanding of the world they are brought into. They hear sounds, then learn to speak those sounds themselves. Their eyes respond to light and color and motion. Their muscles strengthen and allow them to crawl then walk.

At that early stage in their development, there is inevitably a discussion of which parent they look like. Family may say they have their mom's eyes, or their dad's hands. Gracious observers say to the parents, "I see both of you in them." Of course, many children favor one parent more than the other. This is the case with my daughters. Sure, they carry some of my traits, but in their beauty, their appearance favors their mom.

But without fail, people realize that no matter how much the baby resembles the parents, this new life is entirely new, a separate being, a miraculous creation. Their conception and birth is God-ordained in its design. As we believe this about physical birth, so we must accept that spiritual birth is also new and supernatural. What God does in us to get us back to "Eden" is a new birth. It is not putting a new label on something broken, unable to fulfill its original purpose. It is the creation of a new living thing that is able to function as what it was created to be, because it has all it needs to live by divine direction and power.

On Becoming New Creations: The Struggle with the World and Our Flesh

We cannot partially be made a new creature. Our response to God's offer to receive the life of Jesus into our own is an all or nothing, a yes or no, decision. We either ask to be made new, to be born again, or we do not. This explains why we must die before we take on His life. This death of the old self is necessary, for there is no middle ground where we can live in a God-honoring way out of both the old self and the new self at the same time. We cannot follow the desires of our flesh, and at the same time please God without a conflict. What must "give way" in this struggle is our flesh; it must die.

A Wrong View of Pleasing God and Overcoming Our Flesh

If that sounds dramatic, it is. Jesus says we must lose our life to follow Him, and that the way that leads to life is narrow.[90] Living a moral life by our strength of will is not in itself living the narrow way. Lewis explains why attempts to do good do not insure we stay on the narrow way. He says before people become Christians, they "take as starting point our ordinary self with its various desires and interests. We then admit that something else—call it 'morality' or 'decent behavior,' or 'the good of society'—has claims on this self: claims which interfere with its own desires."[91] In other words, because we have a conscience, we are aware we must decide if a demand placed on us is either right or wrong for the good of others and are compelled to choose to act on the good. When we focus on "being good," it places us in a bind. To fulfill the claims that morality or society places on us, we feel we must give up desires that belong to the "old self" because they are wrong, and choose what we feel we must do instead because those desires are seen as "right" by the standard of the moral society. Lewis says, in essence, that as long as we focus on the struggle between our natural desires and the culturally-defined view of right and wrong called morality, we will "either give up trying to be good, or else we become very unhappy indeed."[92]

The burden upon our flesh to meet the demands of "moral goodness," and the demands of other people upon our time, resources, and love is quite taxing. To live in this tension between living to please others while resenting others for not noticing our selfless choices more, can allow us to make a martyr of ourselves. In that case, we make ourselves more problematic to others than if we operated simply by our selfish desires.

To illustrate Lewis' point about meeting the demands of "moral goodness," consider your reaction to a deed done to please someone, when from your viewpoint they don't acknowledge it or even notice it. Maybe you stayed late at work to finish a project that hadn't reached the stated deadline, but you knew its completion would please your boss. And when you informed them you finished it, they said "that's nice," but then changed the subject to point out how your last project didn't meet expectation. Or maybe someone you love is away on a trip, and you surprise them by doing extra work they expressed a desire for, hoping to please them by doing the unexpected. Yet it takes them longer to notice the work than you hoped, or you only receive a quick "thank you" for what you did, and they use the chance to complain about what is still undone. In both cases, we want to give up trying, to feel offended, to get angry, and to resolve within ourselves that it is more satisfying to be selfish than to extend love through actions. We are then tempted to consider God's expectation for how we treat others as impossible. The life Jesus proclaims is that we love God and love others as ourselves. Lewis believes as long as our focus stays on the struggle between our desires and the wishes of others, we take the wrong approach to that struggle.

A Better Way to Becoming New Creations

Lewis envisions a better starting point for becoming a new creation than engaging in the struggle between our old, sinful self and attempts to live by man's definition of morality. Jesus offers us a way out of that war! "Christ says 'Give me all. I don't want so much of your time and so much of your money and so much of your work. I want you. I have not come to torment your natural self, but to kill it. No half measures are any good ... Hand over the whole natural self, all the desires which you think innocent as well as the ones you think wicked—the whole outfit. I will give you a new self instead. In fact, I will give you Myself: my own will shall become yours."[93]

We can't return to the life offered Adam and Eve in Eden by managing this struggle with our old natural desires. This is because our flesh has been corrupted by and enslaved to sin; it cannot receive the life God designed us for.[94] Paul says the spirit and the flesh are at odds.[95] We must "hand over" our old way of viewing how to please God, because Paul says those "in the flesh" cannot please God, and a mind set on the flesh is death.[96] When we hand this "us" over, with all its desires, we get a new "us" in exchange. The glorious truth is that this "new self" is Jesus Himself living through us!

Lewis says handing over to God our whole self is difficult, nearly impossible, but is the only option for becoming new creations, for "it is far easier than what we are all trying to do instead. For what we are trying to do is to remain what we call 'ourselves,' to keep personal happiness as our great aim in life, and yet at the same time be 'good.' We are all trying to let our mind and heart go their own way—centered on money or pleasure or ambition—and hoping, in spite of this, to behave honestly and chastely and humbly. And that is what Christ warned us we could not do … If we want to produce wheat, the change must go deeper than the surface. We need to be plowed up and re-sown."[97] We can't keep walking our own way and walk as a new creation at the same time. We must remove what exists and be re-planted. We must be transformed, reborn.

What a beautiful description of the choice people have faced through the ages, yet it seems so rarely presented in such terms today. If we let our heart and mind go their own way, how can we honestly expect our behavior to imitate God like we are commanded to in Ephesians 5:1? Jesus said we can't serve two masters.[98] Paul says that only one "master" leads us toward God. Either the flesh or the spirit controls us, and only one of them submits itself to God. The mind, which is set on flesh, and on our struggle to satisfy it, keeps a person from fulfilling God's purpose. We can't do enough good things to make our sinful man fulfill all that God has in mind for our life. We must renew our soul and our mind in pursuit of God's will instead of our own will.[99] Walking in His power is not done "in spite of" the inclinations of our heart or mind toward sin. We can't focus on the outside of ourselves, our actions, yet inwardly be full of greed and self-indulgence.[100]

The taking on of Christ, in the form of the new self, is not just a rehabilitation of the old man. Instead, we must gain a new power inside ourselves by plowing up what we once were and allowing God to create something new of us. It is not something we do while holding onto our pursuit of happiness. It is not trying to behave well, nor is it holding onto worldly ambitions or thirst for pleasure. As shown in Paul's letters, this death is truly death to all that we hold dear, all that we think our identity consists of, because it is a new identity that must be put on.

The old self exists no more, and the new self is formed and grows as a new creation. This is essentially what Jesus says in John 12:24–25 "Truly, truly, I say to you, unless a grain of wheat falls into the earth and dies, it remains alone; but if it dies, it bears much fruit."

If we allow our old man to die, the "taking on" of the new self clears the way to produce much fruit in our life. But the measure of that fruit is only found in relation to our understanding of what this death achieves. Through Jesus' death, God has robbed the grave of its power. Dying to self removes the binding influence of the law over us. Paul says "the law of the Spirit of life in Christ Jesus has set you free from the law of sin and death."[101] Just as the law of sin held power over our natural selves, the fear of natural death enslaved us. Jesus removed the sting of death, and took with it any cause for fear.[102] In Hebrews we read of Jesus, "that through death He might render powerless him who had the power of death, that is, the devil, and might free those who through fear of death were subject to slavery all their lives." (Hebrews 2:14 NAS 1995)[103] We don't have to fear slavery to sin and its consequences anymore since we have been set free to be new creations. This is a main theme in Paul's letters, and he sees spreading this message as an essential role for those placing their faith in Jesus and who thus belong to His Body, the Church!

The Mission of God's Children, His Body

Death to our old way of life—living for ourselves and trying to be good—is necessary to find the narrow way to life. This is true for every Christ follower. As a result of our death to self, we operate in a new reality, and have new fruit from the life of Jesus within us. We should not just be content to display the fruit ourselves. The joy we experience as we bear fruit for Him should make us want others to be fruitful also. Believers are responsible to help each other experience new life and its fruit. Lewis says the task of showing mankind this truth, that death of the old self produces new life, is precisely the mission of Jesus' followers, the church Jesus says He is building. The Church's task is to move people to greater Christlikeness.

"The Church exists for nothing else but to draw men into Christ, to make them little Christs. If they are not doing that, all the cathedrals, clergy, missions, sermons, even the Bible itself, are simply a waste of time. God became man for no other purpose."[104]

So Lewis, referring to the incarnation, states that mankind's created purpose is reflecting the image of God. Jesus came as the exact representation of God to produce in us the likeness of His image, to restore us again to our role as image bearers and managers of His earth. Jesus became a man to restore what was given to mankind at original creation, to be like God. Likeness to our Creator and to Jesus, who perfectly reflects the image of God, is the birthright for all who are called by God. The bride of Christ, the Church Jesus says He will build, has as its primary task drawing men and women into the Christlike life, helping them to know their identity as God's children.[105] But in this pursuit of helping others to imitate Christ, believers must show others what God intends the result of this process to be.

What We Are in for

Lewis says there is a reason Jesus told people to count the cost of following Him: God intends to complete the process He began of making us disciples of Christ. "'Make no mistake,' He says, 'if you let me, I will make you perfect. The moment you put yourself in My hands, that is what you are in for. Nothing less, or other, than that. You have free will, and you can push Me away. But if you do not push Me away, understand that I am going to see this job through.'"[106] The process the Father has begun in us by making us a new creation will only reach its end when we are "perfect and complete, lacking in nothing."[107] Though in the long term, God is "satisfied with nothing less than absolute perfection," He, as a good Father, is "delighted with the first feeble, stumbling effort you make tomorrow to do the simplest duty."[108]

God's expectation of perfection should not discourage us when our feeble steps forward feel like failure. Our good Father is pleased when we make choices that reflect the new life inside us. Yet Lewis contends that only *we* stand in the way of God moving us toward likeness to Him.[109] "We may be content to remain what we call 'ordinary people': but He is determined to carry out a quite different plan. To shrink back from that plan is not humility: it is laziness and cowardice. To commit to it is not conceit or megalomania, it is obedience."[110]

We should want everything that God intends for us. So to shrink back from God's full purpose for our redemption is not humility. We can boldly embrace His purpose for us, knowing He tells us to ask Him for our needs, and He will meet them from His rich supply.[111] We are not meant to fail in His purpose. We need to ask Him to reveal His plans for us individually. *That is why understanding we are Made for Eden is so important.* We must not think less of ourselves or our role than what God says is true.[112] We must pursue all God has for us, for it is cowardice to hold back from allowing God to manifest His plans for us. God sees the sin of cowardice as serious.[113]

When God makes us new creations, He makes our spirits new at salvation. In the core of our being, we are newly formed, restored to the image of God. Yet as a new creation, our soul must be perfected through a process, over time. This is why Paul can say we are to be transformed through the renewing of our mind (part of the soul, along with the will and emotions) so we can approve God's will. As we stop conforming to the way of the world, we can test or examine the perfect will of God and find it trustworthy. As we are transformed in our minds, we are renewed in greater likeness to our Creator. We must recognize that the adage that "God is not finished with me yet" is a scriptural idea.[114] Christians are often disillusioned when troubles come their way. Because God is forming us into more patient, or more loving, people than we ever dreamed of being before. We may not understand the process, but that is because we have not yet understood the holiness He means to create in us.

We often don't see the trials we face in this process of sanctification as beneficial. We don't know the "finished product" God has in mind for us as He molds us to be more like Jesus. But when we see ourselves as Made for Eden, designed to live in His presence, and to have His presence actually inside us, we can view ourselves not just as a "fixer upper," but as the beautiful dwelling place of God.

In support of the notion of our perfection as God's goal, consider the analogy of God rebuilding us as though we are a house. At times, we may know what He is up to in the renovation; at other times, we have no clue. This is because God's project is different in scope than we could imagine. "You thought you were going to be made into a decent little cottage: but He is building a palace. He intends to come and live in it Himself."[115] God intends to live inside us, so He refashions us to make his dwelling place worthy and capable of displaying the glory He intends to emanate from it.

TV shows about house transformations are popular with many viewers. They have names like *Fixer Upper* and *Extreme Makeover: Home Edition*. Viewers enjoy seeing the transformation that some hard work and creative vision can do to make a house a home for someone. As special as a transformed home is, what would a home for God to live in look like? The transformation would be "exceedingly abundant beyond all we ask or imagine," for the Creator Himself comes to live there. What God has done in making us new creations is more than replacing some faulty wiring or knocking out a wall to open up the spaces. He transforms us to make us a vessel of honor, set apart as useful to the Master.[116]

The result of God restoring us is that we can do what was impossible before. We become sons of our Father in Heaven.[117] As a result, He tells us to be perfect as He is.[118] This is not a command to do the impossible. He makes us able to obey that command. When He has made us a new creation, we are fully capable of obeying Him. While we will be tempted to revert to old patterns of sinful behavior, sin is no longer our master. Being a new creation also changes our identity. We aren't just His creations; we become sons and daughters, enjoying a new intimacy as family. Again, Lewis says "God became man to turn creatures into sons: not simply to produce better men of the old kind but to produce a new kind of man."[119] Doing His will is to become our highest priority as we learn to think His thoughts, because we have the mind of Christ. In becoming new creatures, our life begins to look more like His, as we follow His will.

Yet the process of losing ourselves does not wipe out the uniqueness God built into us. Rather, it draws it out. We, along with all of God's children, play different parts in His story. He knows our unique role in advancing His purpose because He prepares it for us.[120] We will never be our true selves apart from what He created us to be.

The goal of this chapter was to describe the path back to the life we were created for. Jesus accomplished our renewal to God's purpose in coming to die for sin and to bring us life. But we must also die and become new creatures. We are to reject our own "old" life and surrender to God's ways. Jesus says "For if you choose self-sacrifice and lose your lives for My glory, you will continually discover true life. But if you choose to keep your lives for yourselves, you will forfeit what you try to keep." (Matthew 16:25, TPT)[121]

As we discover true life by losing our own, we become stewards of the kingdom of God as we grow toward our created purpose. We become His stewards by becoming new creations in Him. We put aside the sinful self, the life lived by and for its own desires, in order to be reborn to the life He meant for us. As we mature in our likeness to Him, we become more of the person God specifically had in mind when He created us. If life as a new creation is the key to restoration to Eden, then the relationship with God that results from our new life needs a model. We are to learn from Jesus how His earthly life is an example of the life He came to provide for all of us by His death. As we see how He relates as a Son to His Father, we see how He wants us to relate to the Father as a son.

5

The Life Jesus Led: Eden as the Inheritance of Sons

By the way Jesus lived his life on earth, we can see that mankind's restoration to God's purpose in Eden was on His mind. He lived according to several beliefs about the purpose of His life while on earth.

> ➤ He knew that life would come from His death for all who embraced His victory over sin and death.
> ➤ He knew His obedience to His Father, even death on a cross, would accomplish the reconciliation of God and man, so He submitted to the Father's plan. His obedience culminated in His death on the cross for all mankind's sin. His death conquered sin committed both in the garden and subsequently by mankind throughout all of history.
> ➤ He died as part of a plan to restore us to the God-directed life we were created to live.
> ➤ He came to model what obedience to the Father looks like.

Peter tells us Jesus left us an example so we could follow in His steps.[122] To live as Jesus did, as a Son submitted to the Father's will, is our goal. In doing so, we find the life we were promised, life as our Creator designed. But we can't learn to imitate His life of humble dependence on the Father by following any way but His. Even Jesus' disciples argued about who among them was the greatest, measuring their worth by their own standards. If they were guilty of wrong motives, wrong methods, and wrong actions, we can be sure that we too will be tempted to follow the way of the world.[123] We can be captivated by the flesh to follow our own path in life, unless we discover and live out our true purpose, aided by the power of God working in us.

Jesus as an Example of Living in Relationship to God

The ability to again walk unashamed with God, as Adam and Eve did in the garden, is not achieved by trying harder to be good. It is exhausting trying to please God if we pursue Him from a religious mindset. Though well-meaning in their attempts, religious people try to act better and do more. Jesus knew the danger of separating our relationship with God the Creator from what we do for Him. Because we are already redeemed, the things we do in the pursuit of more likeness to Him are not merit toward salvation, but to express our gratitude for redemption and to glorify our Father and Creator. Jesus called out those who seemed to be missing the point of pursuing life with God. It is not how we look in the eyes of others, but how we look in God's eyes that matters. This is why He attacked the Pharisees. He knew their attempts to obey the letter of the law were not the result of a heart to follow the intent of the spirit of the law. He felt they were truly focused on not being condemned for failure to obey even a small detail of law. Instead of focusing on things God desires, like being just and faithful, they ignored these important things in their focus on avoiding judgment.

In Matthew 23, Jesus speaks "woes" toward those guilty of ignoring what is most vital.

"Woe to you, scribes and Pharisees, hypocrites! For you tithe mint and dill and cumin, and have neglected the weightier provisions of the law: justice and mercy and faithfulness;"[124]

"Woe to you, scribes and Pharisees, hypocrites! For you clean the outside of the cup and of the dish, but inside they are full of robbery and self-indulgence."[125]

"So you, too, outwardly appear righteous to people, but inwardly you are full of hypocrisy and lawlessness."[126]

Jesus said they focused on appearing to obey the law yet had evil inside. By strictly observing laws, yet ignoring the spirit behind them, they were hypocrites. Because they failed to honor the intent behind the law and focused only on strict observance of the letter of the law they were called lawless. The life God meant for us in Eden is much more than trying to make ourselves look righteous. It is not a religious life—of trying to please Him by doing good—but a life guided by His purpose for us. We live for Him as He empowers us to fulfill that purpose. Because Jesus lived according to the Father's purpose, He did not follow every human expectation or request placed on Him. He was not after men's approval. He only wanted to follow His Father's will and purpose. He knew His Father would empower Him to accomplish that purpose.

Why is this important? Because we should not get our direction for life from each other! Only God's standards for a righteous life matter, and Jesus was showing the Pharisees how they fell short. And the example of Jesus' commitment to the Father's will shows that we are meant to live each day in the intimate presence of God, just like they did in the garden. Because of that presence in us and with us, we are directed by Him! Jesus expected His Father to show Him what to do in all situations because He was in relationship with the Father as His child. Confident He would return to Him when He had accomplished all He was sent to do, Jesus listened and obeyed.

Jesus as a Son, Well Pleasing to His Father

Jesus knew He was sent from the Father, and His call was to do the will of God who sent Him. He knew the Father was "well-pleased" with His willingness to be His instrument to rescue His people.

I have the blessing of a family that celebrates well. Birthdays, anniversaries, Father's Day, and all the others are occasions to be together and give thanks for the one being celebrated. The giving of handwritten cards is a special part of those celebrations. Feelings are expressed in those cards which have an effect beyond the useful life of the tangible gift. In many of those cards I have been affirmed as a son, as a dad, and as a husband. And also as a pastor, as a friend, as a son-in-law, as a coworker, I have been edified by those words. There is a part of everyone's core that wants to hear from others "well done, much appreciated, greatly loved."

Father God knows this is important too. He took the moment when Jesus arose from baptism by John, to say over him "this in my beloved Son, in whom I am well-pleased."[127] Again, when Peter offered to build a tabernacle for Jesus, Moses, and Elijah, a voice from heaven said, "This is my beloved Son, with whom I am well pleased; listen to him!"[128] Lest there be any confusion about the unique mission of Jesus in comparison to the Law or the Prophets, the Father clarified that Jesus is the source of new life—listen to Him.

Like the words spoken over Jesus show His relationship to the Father, the words Jesus speaks over us tell who we are and how we figure into the Father's plans. Knowing that He was well-pleasing to the Father, the actions required to fulfill

His call to be Messiah were really nourishment to Him.[129] The reality that sustained Him, as food sustains the body, was to do the Father's will. Following the Father's plan was not burdensome to Jesus. Rather, Jesus said it nourished Him as food does to the body. Adam and Eve saw that the tree was good for food and pleasing to their eye. Instead of making God's will their food and source of their joy, as Jesus would do in the future, they believed the enemy's words. Those words were contrary to what God had spoken to them. Jesus, in calling His Father's will His food, demonstrated that true obedience means obeying Him rather than the voice of another. We cannot live without food very long. Jesus was saying, "I depend on doing what My Father directs Me as much as a body does on food." As Jesus told the devil during His temptation, "Man shall not live on bread alone but on every word that comes out of the mouth of God."[130] Hearing from God is as critical for His children as it was for Jesus!

Willingly Choosing Father's Plan

Jesus also made certain His hearers knew that His commitment to laying down His life was His own choice. We have the same choice to take on the life of Jesus in us. He says in John 10:17–18:

> "For this reason the Father loves Me, because I lay down My life so that I may take it again. "No one has taken it away from Me, but I lay it down on My own initiative. I have authority to lay it down, and I have authority to take it up again. This commandment I received from My Father." (NAS 1995)[131]

Jesus is saying the command, or will, of the Father for Him is to exercise His authority to lay down His life, believing the Father would restore life to Him, which the Father did in the resurrection and ascension.

Knowing His identity allowed Jesus to fulfill the purpose of His Father. John says, "Jesus knew that the Father had given everything into His hands, that He had come from God, and that He was going back to God." (John 13:3 HCSB) [132] Jesus knew His origin was in heaven and His destiny was to return there to reign. Before His incarnation—in fact before time began—He was with the Father. And after His death, resurrection, and ascension, He would be at the Father's right hand.

What did the knowledge of His origin and destiny produce in Jesus? It produced an assurance of His purpose, and a humility in fulfilling it. He could willingly wash the dirty feet of His disciples and show them what serving others is about. He said in John 13:14–15 that if He, their Lord and teacher, washed their feet, they should wash one another's feet. Humility before our Creator is one result of knowing we are made for Eden, and Paul tells us Jesus was the ultimate example of humility. [133]

Living Beyond Human Expectation: What Relating to God as Father Makes Possible for Sons

One important thing Jesus had that we also need is confidence in the Father to exercise His power in response to our faith. I stated that Jesus, because He knew His identity and His purpose, did not follow human expectations placed on Him—even by people He loved dearly. As a Son, He desired most to please His Father, not people. As new creations and stewards with the presence of Jesus in our lives, we can have faith that God will move. Confidence in our Father allows us to rise above human expectation and trust God to move in a situation the way it fulfills His purposes. One narrative that demonstrates Jesus' ability to focus only on fulfilling His Father's will and not human need or expectation is in John 11 about Lazarus.

> "Now a certain man was sick, Lazarus of Bethany, the village of Mary and her sister Martha. It was the Mary who anointed the Lord with ointment, and wiped His feet with her hair, whose brother Lazarus was sick. So the sisters sent *word* to Him, saying, "Lord, behold, he whom You love is sick." But when Jesus heard *this*, He said, "This sickness is not to end in death, but for the glory of God, so that the Son of God may be glorified by it." Now Jesus loved Martha and her sister and Lazarus. So when He heard that he was sick, He then stayed two days *longer* in the place where He was. Then after this He said to the disciples, "Let us go to Judea again." The disciples said to Him, "Rabbi, the Jews were just now seeking to stone You, and are You going there again?" (John 11:1-8, NAS 1995)[134]

First, Jesus was confident that He could "awaken" Lazarus from death, so He delayed going to be with him until he was dead. "'Our friend Lazarus has fallen asleep; but I go, so that I may awaken him out of sleep.' The disciples then said to Him, Lord, if he has fallen asleep, he will recover. Now Jesus had spoken of his death, but they thought that He was speaking of literal sleep. So Jesus then said to them plainly, 'Lazarus is dead, and I am glad for your sakes that I was not there, so that you may believe; but let us go to him.'" (John 11:11-15, NAS 1995)[135] Martha then said to Jesus, "Lord, if You had been here, my brother would not have died. Even now I know that whatever You ask of God, God will give You." Jesus said to her, "Your brother will rise again." Martha said to Him, "I know that he will rise again in the resurrection on the last day." Jesus said to her, "I am the resurrection and the life; he who believes in Me will live even if he dies, and everyone who lives and believes in Me will never die. Do you believe this?" (John 11:21-26, NAS1995)[136]

Then Mary arrives. John says of this moment "when Mary came where Jesus was, she saw Him and fell at His feet, saying to Him, 'Lord, if You had been here, my brother would not have died.' When Jesus therefore saw her weeping, and the Jews who came with her *also* weeping, He was deeply moved in spirit and was troubled ..." (John 11:32-35, NAS 1995)[137] So both Martha and Mary believe that if Jesus had been there, their brother would not have died. Jesus responds to the sisters differently, but to neither does he say, "I know you wanted me here quicker, I am sorry I was late." Perhaps the two days He lingers before going are spent largely in prayer with His Father, to discern what the Father's will was in the matter. The fact that Jesus knew Lazarus had died before he had arrived to witness it is further evidence of communion with His Father.[138] Because He is resolute that this sickness is not to end in death, He can say He is glad He was not there before the death.[139]

John then presents the miracle of Jesus calling Lazarus back to life. "Jesus said to her, 'Did I not say to you that if you believe, you will see the glory of God?' They removed the stone. Then Jesus raised His eyes, and said, "Father, I thank You that You have heard Me. I knew that You always hear Me; but because of the people standing around I said it, so that they may believe that You sent Me.' When He had said these things, He cried out with a loud voice, 'Lazarus, come forth.'" (John 11:41-43, NAS 1995)[140] Jesus knew that His Father was strengthening Him to fulfill His earthly purpose, which included healing the sick and raising the dead.[141] In raising Lazarus, Jesus was also preparing His followers for His own death and subsequent resurrection, by showing that as God's power could raise Lazarus, Jesus would also be raised and return to heaven. But Jesus was not going to act based on any person's timing or understanding of what was possible. Jesus says in John 8:

"When you lift up the Son of Man, then you will know that I am *He,* and I do nothing on My own initiative, but I speak these things as the Father taught Me. And He who sent Me is with Me; He has not left Me alone, for I always do the things that are pleasing to Him." (John 8:28-29, NAS 1995)[142]

Jesus' mindset was not moved by the facts, even the fact that Lazarus was dead. He trusted in the truth that His Father would answer what Jesus asked of Him. That belief made the miraculous possible! Jesus said He knows the Father always hears Him. But so those present know that the Father sent Him, for their benefit He thanks the Father for hearing Him."[143] His mind and heart were focused on doing only what He saw His Father doing.[144]

Stewarding Our Faith

There is a passage that demonstrates the link between the restoration of mankind's created purpose and the exercise of his faith. Often we take Luke 17, where the apostles ask Jesus to increase their faith, and apply the passage to argue that more faith is necessary to fulfill our God-given purpose. Jesus answers the disciples' request by pointing to the relationship of servant to master. Faith is exercised by doing what the master commands. Jesus demonstrates that He took on the form of a servant and from that position, willingly did what His Father led Him to do, which was an exercise of faith.[145] In light of how Jesus sees acting on what the master commands, we need to reexamine what Jesus is saying in Luke 17 about faith.

In Luke 17:6-10, Jesus said, "If you had faith like a mustard seed, you would say to this mulberry tree, 'Be uprooted and be planted in the sea'; and it would obey you. Which of you, having a slave plowing or tending sheep, will say to him when he has come in from the field, 'Come eat, and *properly* clothe yourself and serve me while I eat and drink; and afterward you may eat and drink'? He does not thank the slave because he did the things which were commanded, does he? So you too, when you do all the things which are commanded you, say, 'We are unworthy slaves; we have done *only* that which we ought to have done.'"(NAS 1995)[146]

Proximity to the Power, Not Amount of Faith, Determines the Outcome

Jesus' answer to his disciples in Luke 17 reflects His conviction that they don't need more faith to accomplish what He desires them to do because we serve a good Master who has told us to ask persistently of Him. Much has been written about the "faith of a mustard seed," and many explanations seem to miss the point. You have a relationship with Father God, the One who made creation, and you are a co-heir of life alongside Jesus. Our proximity to the power and authority that called the world into being gives us authority. Jesus says we have authority because we are under His authority. He commends the centurion for understanding this. We should expect results when we pray in faith because we are appealing to Jesus' authority over the situation. He promises we have enough authority to bring results when we exercise the authority He gives us by praying in His name.[147]

Jesus has just proclaimed to them an astonishing reality. Jesus here tells them that the ability to speak to creation rests with them, just as the winds and waves obeyed Him! Possibly the apostles are picking up their chins off the ground at this point. Luke does not tell us their reaction to Jesus' statement. Based on what Jesus says next, perhaps they were feeling full of themselves in this newly proclaimed authority. Jesus tells them a slave/master parable. His point seems to be that there is natural order in place between a servant and a master. In meeting the master's needs, the servant ought not to expect special commendation for doing what his position dictates he must do. They ought to view such service as doing what is required. Some translations of this passage say the servants have only done their duty.[148]

In telling them to exercise their faith, Jesus has given them much authority, much more than they could have realized. But it's not power for power's sake. It is a creature doing what their creator meant for them to do and to be. The glory of the "moving of mountains," or of trees being uprooted and cast into the sea, is not something the master should thank them for or commend as special. It is what is expected of us as a servant of the Most High God. Yet the moving of mountains is not based on the measure of our faith. It is because we live by the faith of Jesus, who lives in us. These are Paul's words to believers in Galatians 2:20. We live by His faith, and believe that He who created all things is also our Father. And He wants us to believe in His goodness and His willingness to answer prayers offered in faith. These prayers carry authority with Him because they expect the desired outcomes. We were created for that kind of authority and to pray that kind of prayer.

Faith in a Good Master

The best way to interpret Jesus' instruction about the faith to forgive those who repent in Luke 17, based on how Jesus replies to their request for Him to give them more faith, is this. Exercising faith is simply doing our duty to our Master, doing what we were created to do. It's not that they need more faith; they just need to realize the authority He has given them, and exercise their faith based on that. If they will do so, they can overcome obstacles in their way. And they can be servants of the Most High God who do what is expected of them. He assures the servant who uses his talents well and multiplies them that he will receive a commendation at the end, "well done, good and faithful servant." (Matthew 25:23 NKJV)[149] So we know the parable in Luke 17 should not be interpreted to mean that no praise or gratitude can be expected for doing what God expects. We are not, in God's economy, "good for nothing slaves" when we obey, doing what is expected. The only servant characterized by Jesus as worthless is *he who misunderstands the true heart and nature of His master and thus fails to attempt what is expected.*[150] What He is saying is we shouldn't perform our duty out of expectation of what we will receive. Rather, we do what is expected of citizens of heaven in order to honor the King who loved us and gave Himself for us.[151] While on earth, we can confidently move forward in obedience to what He tells us to accomplish. When we enter our eternal rest, we get the final evaluation of how well we became imitators of God. We will see how well we lived as beloved children, and how well we understood that God is a Father who longs to give good gifts to His children.[152] Did we so fully know His nature that we longed to imitate Him?

Sadly, many people on earth see traits exhibited in their parents that they don't want to imitate. In fact, they have vowed to never be like that parent or parents. But Paul's command in Ephesians 5:1 assumes that if we understand the nature of God and embrace our position as sons and daughters of a Father infinitely worthy of our praise, we will honor Him by imitating His character. To pursue being like the most glorious being in the universe, and to be viewed as growing ever more like Him, honors the One who made us. We bring joy to Him and take part in His plan for mankind when we exhibit more of His likeness and less of our own. When we engage in the works He set out before us, we are able to share His joy.[153]

The Responsibility of Servants: Persist in the Master's Business over Time

Earlier in the book we saw where a wrong view of God takes us. What was Jesus seeking to show about persistence in trusting the Master? No matter how intimate of a relationship God intends for us through Jesus, the character of a servant is tested by time. In Matthew 25, Jesus says the master returned "after a long time." What had the servant done during this long absence? Was trust in the nature of the Master strong enough to keep the servant active in his work? For the first two servants in the parable, such trust in the master, and in the master's desire to honor that trust, was firmly in place. The last servant, driven by fear, did not "put to work" what he was given. The child of God commits grievous sin by holding back his talents out of fear. It is not an exercise of faith when the Master returns after a long absence to offer back to Him the very talents He gave us without having multiplied them. Jesus says the master wishes the servant had at least followed the shrewd ways of the world—to earn interest on the talent. *To let the talent sit idle is to reject the gift.*

Even if Scripture convinces someone they are Made for Eden and empowered by God to fulfill their purpose, their view of God's nature can prevent them from wanting that gift or being motivated to undergo the necessary denial of self. The pursuit of a life that is made a new creation by Jesus, indwelt by His Spirit, and brings glory to the Father, depends on some assumptions about the nature of God.

False assumptions:

> God doesn't love me unless I am morally good (make right choices).
> God only wants me in His family if I make Him look good.
> God only includes the strong and the righteous in His family.
> God has His favorites, to whom He shows favor, and I can never be one of those.

True nature of the Father:

> He is a rewarder of those who diligently seek Him.
> He does not tempt us to do evil.
> He does exceedingly abundantly beyond all we ask or imagine.

So how do we receive God's gift of new life and develop it so that we multiply its value as the good servant does with the talent? What does it look like to do what we were created to do? How do we add to our "talents," to use the words of the parable? Living according to His plan for us and multiplying what "talents" He has given us starts with realizing we were dead and are now alive. In living out that plan, we discover it has all been prepared for us beforehand! He knew before we were "made alive," before our natural birth even, what "aliveness" would produce in us.

Jesus' Kingdom and Eden

Jesus fulfilled by His sacrifice the promise that by becoming new creations we can return to Eden. He came to remove the separation sin created between us and God, between us and His purpose. He will return to earth a second time as King. At His first coming, He proclaimed that His kingdom had begun. Both Jesus and his forerunner, John, spoke of the kingdom of heaven being near.[154] Jesus spoke in parables of what the kingdom is like. Jesus preached the kingdom to declare who He is, the King, and what He came to do, which is to complete the Father's plan for the restoration of all things. He will take His place as the King, and as prophesied, we will rule with Him.

The Worth of the Kingdom

If Jesus is King and is our example for how to live by God's plan, it is important to understand what He rules over. What is the kingdom of God? And why is it so valuable? Why did Jesus speak of "kingdom" so many more times than He did salvation? Why does serving His kingdom deserve the full investment of all we are? If we want to live how we were made to live, we must understand what Jesus says the context for "eternal life" is. For Jesus, the context is being ruler servants of His kingdom. "A kingdom is a realm, quite simply, where the king's word has full authority. What the king desires is what happens. God's "kingdom come" means that His will is done "on earth as it is in heaven."[155] The will of God is always done in heaven, for He alone rules there. The Apostle John says we should know we are children of God as the ruler of this world is the evil one.[156] Why does John place these truths together? Because making every effort to foster the will of our Father being done on earth "as it is in heaven" is our responsibility. It is also our privilege as children of God.

Proof that Jesus' kingdom is advancing around us is when the will of the King, Jesus, is done here as in heaven. The Gospels show us that when the kingdom message was proclaimed, lives are changed.

> "Jesus was going throughout all Galilee, teaching in their synagogues and proclaiming the gospel of the kingdom, and healing every kind of disease and every kind of sickness among the people. The news about Him spread throughout all Syria; and they brought to Him all who were ill, those suffering with various diseases and pains, demoniacs, epileptics, paralytics; and He healed them."(Matthew 4:23-24 NAS1995)[157]

Yet the fact that we are brothers of King Jesus, loved so completely by God, is truly joyful news.

Parables of the Kingdom's Worth

This is why Jesus told parables like the one in Matthew 13:44–46 about treasure buried in the field, and the pearl of great price. With such a great reward for persevering in the good He prepared for us, it is worth everything we have in order to pursue it. The parable says, "the Kingdom of heaven is like," not "salvation is like." Jesus, when He refers to the kingdom, is describing more than "going to heaven when you die." The reward of heaven would be enough to sacrifice "all" for, like the man in the parable who buys the field, but that's not the entirety of His offer. Jesus describes "eternal life" as including benefits in this life with heaven as the future reward for those who sacrifice for Him in this life. The reward is for those who take up their cross and follow Him.

While on earth, our reward is in knowing that the will of our Father is done. When it is done, He receives honor. We get the satisfaction of fulfilling our purpose. We have the fruits of the spirit in greater measure which produces their own reward in our relationships and our witness. These fruits make us more like Jesus and enable us to love God and others better. Our witness becomes attractive, and people want what we have.

In Luke 18, Jesus says. "Truly I say to you, there is no one who has left house or wife or brothers or parents or children, for the sake of the kingdom of God, who will not receive many times as much *at this time* and *in the age to come*, eternal life."[158] Jesus envisions those who sacrifice things to serve the kingdom receiving "many times as much at this time." In this life, now, there is blessing in serving the King and His kingdom. And in the future, in the age to come, we will receive eternal life. The focus now is on the kingdom's advance. One day, in the age to come, the crown that is reserved in heaven for those who long for Jesus' appearing and who honored the King of the kingdom will be ours.[159]

Why does Jesus discuss the kingdom? Jesus has an inheritance as Son of the Creator. He was present and involved at creation, and He knows those who are redeemed by His death will inherit a place in this kingdom. They were made to rule; and in His kingdom, they will.

Jesus' Relationship with the Father Puts Our Enemy in His Rightful Place

Jesus clearly understood that coming to earth meant God's promise to Israel of a Messiah was fulfilled. Through His death He offered the payment that redeemed us from sin's curse and restored man to His inheritance. But this sacrifice also several other things possible that are important to the return to Eden.

First, Jesus knows the Father's business, and He commits to that purpose. "For whatever the Father does, these things the Son also does in the same way. For the Father loves the Son, and shows him all things He Himself is doing."[160] Through Jesus living His life in us, we too can know the Father's business.

Second, because He hears from the Father, and obeys what He hears, He *models for us* walking with God as a Son and a friend. In John 15:15, Jesus says He now calls the disciples friends, "because all things that I have heard from my Father I have made known to you."[161] Because Jesus has been shown everything the Father is doing (John 5:20), and He makes everything known to His followers, *then we can know what the Father is showing us to do.* Adam and Eve knew what God wanted because they were in His presence as He walked with them in the cool of the day. As Jesus depended on the Father inside Him doing His work, as followers of Jesus, we will depend on God working in us because He is living through us, to produce what is pleasing to Him.[162]

Third, Jesus does the same things as He sees the Father doing. This demonstrates His love for the Father, and thus prevents Satan from having a foothold in Jesus by which to tempt Him. John 14 says, "I will not speak much more with you, for the ruler of the world is coming, and he has nothing in regard to Me; but so that the world may know that I love the Father, I do exactly as the Father commanded Me."[163] Jesus was living in such obedience to the Father that His enemy could not distract Jesus from His purpose. This is a very powerful truth for us about righteous living and its impact on spiritual warfare. If we resist the devil, he flees, looking for someone else to devour. Jesus would not empower the enemy by speaking words that didn't reflect faith.

In summary, Jesus called us into His kingdom, and to a commitment to His Father's will. We are invited to join the reigning King in what He is doing in the earth. And to do that, we must live by the power produced by Him living inside us.

6

Christ in Us as Eden Fulfilled

While on earth as the Son of Man, Jesus followed the Father's direction closely, obeying His voice as we all were meant to do. Peter expresses belief in Jesus as our example. In doing what was right, what His Father directed, and suffering for it, Peter says Jesus left us an example to follow. As we follow Him, we entrust the outcome of our steps of faith to God.[164] Jesus says in following Him, we take up our cross. This involves rejecting our old life and surrendering to His way. This chapter discusses how to do that, and how this rejection—and the surrender that must follow—allows us to fulfill and enjoy our Eden purpose.

In Matthew 16, Jesus said to his disciples,

"If you truly want to follow me, you should at once completely reject and disown your own life. And you must be willing to share My cross and experience it as your own, as you continually surrender to My ways. For if you choose self-sacrifice and lose your lives for My glory, you will continually discover true life." (Matthew 16:24-25 TPT)[165]

When we reject our old way of living by our flesh, Jesus can live His life in us by the Spirit. This is required for our return to our created purpose, and for the restoration of our relationship with God. Jesus showed by His obedience to

His Father's voice that He came to earth in order to die. He understood that His death would remove the estrangement from God created by sin so that all mankind could have a close relationship with God like He enjoyed. He made Himself an example for us—of yielding to the Father's plan. His actions demonstrate the power of a crucified life of obedience to the Father's will. Because he embraced Jesus' death and resurrection as the payment for sin and the path back to the Father, Paul became the apostle who proclaimed and demonstrated the life yielded to God.

Paul understood the message of Jesus to be the "mystery" of God's will that had for ages been hidden, but that God was now unveiling. The revelation of this mystery is the fulfillment of God's plan to reconcile mankind to Himself. This plan is to redeem them from Adam and Eve's original sin, which brought the curse of sin upon all people. Before considering Paul's description of the crucified life, a look at Paul's life shows how much his approach to pleasing God changed when he became an apostle of this message.

Paul's Call to Be God's Messenger

For Paul to become the apostle of the surrendered life required God's intervention because he was so zealously opposed to followers of Christ. A look at Paul's background helps us understand the reason his call was so remarkable. Paul was miraculously spoken to by God and called to be His messenger to the gentile nations that had not been taught about Jesus. With his dedication to Judaism and his passionate persecution of Christians, he was an unlikely choice to be apostle to the gentiles. Before God appeared to him, he was present at the stoning of Stephen, where he saw how committed to Christ's purpose on earth His followers were. As God did with Moses and David, He again chose an unlikely vessel to accomplish His purposes. With his deep knowledge of Jewish history, and his revelation that Jesus was the promised Messiah, Paul was truly the man to bring gentiles into God's family of faith.

Because he followed the voice of God on the Damascus Road, Paul became an apostle by divine call, and he began to be led by God's Spirit. The first message out of his mouth was that Jesus is the Son of God.[166] He came in human form to earth not only to destroy the works of the devil, but to offer atonement to the Father for the original sin committed in the garden.[167] Jesus made Himself nothing by becoming human, as Paul described in Philippians 2. In so doing, He died that we might live under the direction and empowerment of the Father. We are able to live according to His purpose and by His power because we have been cleansed and made right with God by Jesus.

Another way to summarize what Paul says about Jesus is that He experienced death on behalf of all mankind, and through this death and resurrection, we can live resurrected lives, with new power and authority. But Paul's understanding of the life Jesus secured for us requires a change of thinking.

Paul's Understanding of the Life Jesus Modeled

To see how radical this call to a surrendered life was for Paul, we see his description of his own life. Paul was a devoted Jew, committed to doing all things according to Jewish law. He wanted to be the most faithful follower of Judaism, as fully a Hebrew as any among the Jews. But Paul realized that striving toward this full devotion did not qualify him to experience the life with God that Jesus came to bring. He says in Philippians

3, "although I myself might have confidence even in the flesh. If anyone else has a mind to put confidence in the flesh, I far more: circumcised the eighth day, of the nation of Israel, of the tribe of Benjamin, a Hebrew of Hebrews; as to the Law, a Pharisee; as to zeal, a persecutor of the church; as to the righteousness which is in the Law, found blameless."[168]

If anyone could justifiably put confidence in the actions of his flesh to produce righteousness, Paul would have qualified. But he says he intentionally refused to let all these distinguishing marks of his life either measure his righteousness or justify confidence in himself. Instead, he became part of the "true circumcision."[169] What does Paul mean by laying aside his "confidence in the flesh?" He claims there is a better life available to him: the Christ-empowered life. This is the life God had in mind in Eden. It was the life being offered through the sacrifice of Jesus for sin. It is a life resulting from the crucifixion of our old identity. Paul wished to define that life for all future believers in Jesus as the Christ.

Key Scriptures for Understanding Christ's Life in Us

The New Covenant promises that God living inside us, empowering us to do His will, is how He restores the original purpose He gave us at creation. By the death of Christ, the curse of sin over us is atoned for, and there is a rebirth, or re-creation, into God's original intention. God's promise is that this rebirth is secured by Jesus' death, resurrection, and ascension. Once reborn, we are again able to steward creation as children of God.

By embracing the atoning sacrifice of Jesus as the payment for sin, Paul shows that the kind of life the new Covenant offers requires yielding our lives to the One who died for us.

But it's not just that we admit our attempts at being righteous are not enough for our redemption. It means that our old self must die to break sin's hold on us. In his letter to the Galatians, there is a verse that reflects the promised reality that our old identity is crucified on the cross of Jesus and we get a new life that Jesus lives through us.

"I have been crucified with Christ; and it is no longer I who live, but Christ lives in me; and the *life* which I now live in the flesh I live by faith in the Son of God, who loved me and gave Himself up for me."[170]

Another translation says,

"My old identity has been co-crucified with Messiah and no longer lives; *for the nails of His cross crucified me with him*. And now the essence of this new life is no longer mine, for the Anointed One lives His life through me-*we live in union as one*! My new life is empowered by the faith of the Son of God who loves me so much that He gave Himself for me, and dispenses His life into mine." (Galatians 2:20 TPT)[171]

Jesus lived obedient to the Father's will. Because of His obedience, once He died to redeem us, by our faith in His faithfulness, we are made righteous. In the Father's eyes, the "me" that followed the way of this world is now done away with.

Based on this verse, something must shift in our thinking about what "accepting Jesus" really means. It is far more than seeking forgiveness of sin. It's a whole new way of viewing what God meant for our lives to be and to accomplish. It means not only did He pay to get us back to a life with God, but He empowers the new life we have received. The focus of salvation is not avoiding hell, but what we become when Jesus lives through and in us, and how that reflects the reason He created us. Paul says in this transformation, we have been put to death with Christ. The self we may have focused on improving is no longer in control.[172] It dies, and our spirit is made perfect. The resulting existence is by Jesus, for Jesus, and with Jesus, because He lives His life inside of us.

The "death of self" Paul preaches has appeared in the Bible before. Jesus spoke of losing one's life in order to find it in John 12. His analogy is a wheat seed dying so it produces fruit. Jesus says, "Truly, truly, I say to you, unless a grain of wheat falls into the earth and dies, it remains alone; but if it dies, it bears much fruit. He who loves his life loses it, and he who hates his life in this world will keep it to life eternal."[173] If our minds and hearts are focused on money or pleasure or ambition, we are not able to live according to Jesus' desire for us. These pursuits only carry us further from a crucified life.

The example Jesus lived of dying to self, of humility in spite of His divinity, is truly mind-blowing. Jesus was involved in creation, yet He humbled Himself to become a created one, a Son of Man. Even as I write these words, I am reminded of ways I still want to be recognized, valued, and honored. In my mind, I desire Jesus to live His life through me, to count whatever gain I have as loss. But I know I have miles to go to really imitate the "death to self" that Jesus exhibited while on earth. He was spit on, bruised, and pierced. I have not been. Jesus set aside what others desired from Him with only the acclaim of His Father as His goal. I still put undue weight on what others want of me.

But that is why the words of Jesus offering rest are so powerful. He doesn't ask us to try harder to be worthy of His power working in us. He asks us to take up His way and learn from Him.

"Come to Me, all of you who are weary and burdened, and I will give you rest. All of you, take up My yoke and learn from Me, because I am gentle and humble in heart, and you will find rest for yourselves. For My yoke is easy and My burden is light." (Matthew 11:28-30 HCS)[174]

This is a promise from Jesus that Paul echoes in his descriptions of the surrendered new life in Him. This promise is that He did not come to create burdens for men. He lives in us, not to increase our burden, but to give us rest from all that wearies us.

Paul states the gospel in a nutshell, that Jesus gave Himself up for mankind, then chooses to live His life through them. Jesus was both the sacrifice for, and the initiator of, "new life." He died so He could live in and through us. But He also, as the Firstborn of Creation, was the first example of a man who lived fully at the Father's direction. In embracing His death, we crucify the old us and take on something far better, the life of one who was purchased by God in Jesus. Once our sin nature is crucified and we become new creations, He again appoints us to His original purpose. When we focus on that purpose intently, we are living by His grace and for His pleasure. Paul goes on in his letter to question the Galatians' state of mind, as he believes they have lost their focus on Jesus and on the purpose of redemption, and focused on their own knowledge.

Faith in Jesus, Not Works, as the Source of New life

Paul realizes that as Adam and Eve were deceived by the accuser, so were the Galatians captivated by a message of vanity and selfishness. In Adam and Eve's context, the deception was that eating from the tree would make them like God. In Galatia, there was a belief that keeping law was the way to earn God's favor.

Paul's key verse about faith and the new life in Jesus is in Galatians 2:20. The verses just prior are Paul's defense against this belief that righteousness comes through the law. In Galatians 2:15–16, Paul says,

> "we know very well that we are not set right with God by rule-keeping but only through personal faith in Jesus Christ. How do we know? We tried it-and we had the best system of rules the world has ever seen! Convinced that no human being can please God by self-improvement, we believed in Jesus as the Messiah so that we might be set right before God by trusting in the Messiah, not by trying to be good." (MSG)[175]

Paul's larger point about law here is that because we died to law through our identification with the death of Jesus, we are freed from the attempt to please God by keeping the Law. Jesus perfectly fulfilled the law, and by His death, His fulfillment is all we need to be right with God. We are not under law, but under grace.[176] Jesus already took the curse of sin upon Himself on the cross, and we don't add anything to the atoning work He did in order to get free from the penalty of sin. Because our "putting on Jesus" reflects a death of self, there is freedom or release from our previous existence.[177] We don't get the life of Jesus—the God-empowered and Father-glorifying kind of life—by working for it. We can't earn it; He gives it.[178] We don't crucify ourselves, but Paul says we have become crucified because Christ died for us and rose again.[179] For those who believe and live like Galatians 2:20 is a reality, it's not about proving anything to God or to others. To live crucified is to live by His power, having been given life by the same Spirit who raised Christ from the dead.

Paul's Desire for Resurrection Power

Paul understood that to experience all God has for a believer, we must die to the old self, to the old way of viewing righteousness. We see proof of this where he told the Philippian church that he considered all that was "gain" in the eyes of others concerning his righteousness ("as to the law, a Pharisee, as to the righteousness which is in the Law, found blameless") as loss. Paul believed the righteousness Jesus secured for him surpassed all he could achieve. Paul wanted what Jesus offers: His power operating through his life.

After Paul counts all that as loss, he says, "And I continually long to know the wonders of Jesus more fully and to experience the overflowing power of his resurrection working in me. I will be one with him in his sufferings and I will be one with him in his death."[180] To understand the power of Jesus' sinless life, and the power we are given by His resurrection, are for Paul part of "knowing Him." So is appreciating His suffering at the hands of sinful people a criminal's death. Paul's great desire is to experience the overflowing power of Jesus' resurrection working in him.

Modern believers have also longed to know the power of Jesus' resurrected life that Paul sought to understand. Pastor David Wilkerson was one such seeker. He described his struggle to understand being crucified and the powerful life that follows such a decision. "I must know what it means to die … O Lord, crucify me. Let me die. Let me live the crucified life."[181] After praying this, he "tried to imagine the suffering, the shame, the pain that Christ endured in my behalf."[182] Instead, he felt the words of Jesus. "It is finished! His death is my death. I am dead with Christ … Thanks to Him the following truths that I had never fully understood now began to become real. Our crucifixion is completed—it is over—when we with Christ on our cross can cry out to the whole world 'It is finished!' We must recognize once and for all that Jesus completed the work-that it is not ours but His."[183]

Wilkerson's breakthrough in understanding being co-crucified with Jesus, and his resulting new life, is that it requires us to say Jesus has finished that work for us. He refers to Romans 8:11, which says, "Yes, God raised Jesus to life! And since God's Spirit of Resurrection lives in you, he will also raise your dying body to life by the same Spirit that breathes life into you!" (TPT)[184] The same Holy Spirit who raised Jesus from the dead makes us alive, as we *consider ourselves* dead to sin and alive to God. Our job is to say "yes" to God's work in us, to believe that in doing so our old self was crucified with Him and our new life is lived by this resurrection power! The reason is stated in Galatians 2:20. He dispenses His life into ours!

Paul realized with Jesus living through us we can accomplish what He sets out for us to do! He says "It has become my inspiration and passion in ministry to *labor with a tireless intensity, with his power flowing through me ...*" (Colossians 1:28-29 TPT)[185] We labor to share His goodness with others, and do so with His power, free from condemnation. Once we are co-crucified with Jesus, "the case is closed. There remains no accusing voice of condemnation against those who are joined in life-union with Jesus."[186] The enemy cannot reverse the work of Jesus that freed us from sin and its penalty: death!

We don't have to struggle with efforts to appear righteous because we have received Jesus' life. Wilkerson sees crucifixion as the path to real life. "Crucifixion is the act that brings about the resurrected life."[187] When we are tempted to believe our old self has not died, we should remember that Paul says, "I have been (already) crucified with Christ."[188] Because our struggle to be good enough has ended with our crucifixion, there is no more striving to earn salvation on our own merits. At the same time there is no more condemnation for us on account of sin, because we trust in Jesus, who met the Father's expectations for our redemption. Paul's conclusion is that the death of our old self means that our flesh can no longer rule over us. Jesus, not our flesh, should be master over our thoughts and actions.

This is what Paul is trying to describe through Galatians 2:20 and his descriptions of Jesus' power working through us. He says that as Jesus died to sin's power so He could please the Father, so we have been crucified to its power. With His life at work inside us, we learn to obey the Father as a result of our union with Jesus.

"For by His sacrifice He died to sin's power once and for all, but He now lives continuously for the Father's pleasure. So let it be the same way with you! Since you are now joined with him, you must continually view yourselves as dead and unresponsive to sin's appeal while living daily for God's pleasure in union with Jesus, the Anointed One." (Romans 6:10-11 TPT)[189]

We must view our old self as dead and therefore deposed as ruler over our thoughts and actions.[190] The result of having been crucified with Jesus is that we live daily for His pleasure and purpose, and by His power, we resist our old way of thinking that led us into sin.

Paul's Life: Crucified to Self, Resurrected to Life

Paul was not concerned about adverse circumstances as he pursued God's purpose among the gentiles. Paul knew that having been crucified to follow Jesus meant living by His power. And that power enabled him to overcome any hard circumstance. In 2 Corinthians, Paul says others are boasting of their service in Corinth; Paul feels he must defend his service to Jesus.

"Are they servants of Christ? I speak as if insane-I more so; in far more labors, in far more imprisonments, beaten times without number, often in danger of death. Five times I received from the Jews thirty-nine lashes. Three times I was beaten with rods, once I was stoned, three times I was shipwrecked, a night and a day I have spent in the deep. I have been on frequent journeys, in dangers from rivers, dangers from robbers, dangers from my countrymen, dangers from the Gentiles, dangers in the city, dangers in the wilderness, dangers on the sea, dangers among false brethren; I have been in labor and hardship, through many sleepless nights, in hunger and thirst, often without food, in cold and exposure. Apart from such external things, there is the daily pressure on me of concern for all the churches."(2 Corinthians 11:24–28 NAS 1995)[191]

Paul made tremendous sacrifices to carry the message of Jesus to the known world. Yet it did not produce pride in him for he saw himself as co-crucified with Jesus. Those hardships—even death—were not Paul's focus. His goal was for the body of Christ to follow Jesus! In 2 Corinthians 12, Paul described an experience in heaven where sacred secrets were shared. They were so holy, he was not allowed to repeat them. He said *that* is worth boasting about. But he did not boast. Paul's belief was that he who boasts should boast in the Lord.[192] Paul knew that the goal of his life was to proclaim the risen Jesus, who Himself suffered at the hands of sinful men to provide our redemption. In the pursuit of that goal, no hardships were too great to prevent Paul from fulfilling his ministry.

Paul's Singular Focus

Because Paul saw his life not as his own but as belonging to and given power by Jesus, he was intensely focused on what God called him to do. That focus produced confidence within him to fulfill God's purpose for him. In a number of passages, Paul showed he valued his mission to the gentiles more than his own life.

> ➤ Philippians 1:21—to live is Christ, and to die is gain.
> ➤ Acts 20:24—But I do not consider my life of any account as dear to myself, so that I may finish my course and the ministry which I received from the Lord Jesus, to testify solemnly of the gospel of the grace of God.

Paul had reached the place where death did not scare him. If he died, he would be with Jesus. He says in Philippians 1 that he is hard-pressed between life and death. To be with Jesus is better. But while he labored for their sake, he knew Jesus was in him! To finish the course God lays out for us requires following our Master. Paul was basing his whole future on a new understanding of our Master. God had become man so we could be restored as heirs of a promise, restored unto an inheritance that is reserved for us and that won't fade away. We must set our thinking on that inheritance, for it involves our lives being "hidden" in Jesus, Who saved us.

Setting Our Minds on God

In Colossians 3:1-4, Paul says "Since, then, you have been raised with Christ, set your hearts on things above, where Christ is seated at the right hand of God. Set your minds on things above, not on earthly things. For you died, and your life is now hidden with Christ in God. When Christ, who is your life, appears, you will appear with Him in glory." (NIV)[193]

Paul says Jesus *is our life*. Not just living in us, but *our life*. He lives; we have died. When we put away the part of us that wants to operate independently of our Father and Master, we can fully experience that life. We used to serve sin as our master. Paul says we were enslaved.[194] But then the old self was crucified; it died to sin by the sacrifice of Jesus! We walk in a new way—which is really the original way—of God being our everything. This new way involves new thinking. Instead of worry, we can focus on the true and lovely.

> "So keep your thoughts continually fixed on all that is authentic and real, honorable and admirable, beautiful and respectful, pure and holy, merciful and kind. And fasten your thoughts on every glorious work of God, praising him always." (Philippians 4:8 TPT)[195]

Now that we have been liberated from sin and made God our master, good fruit results from our union with Him. We receive from Him eternal life, not death.

The New Man is Made According to God

Before sharing examples of lives living by resurrection power, one verse from Paul shows us that the new man is a fulfillment of Eden. God formed Adam from dust by His unique power as Creator. Our new nature likewise is formed by His creative power. The new man is not *our* work; it is God's creative work, a new and "beyond the natural" realm of being. We become new creations because God has re-created us as He intended us to be in Eden. This new creation reflects a spiritual reality that carries a natural consequence for our time on earth.

This new man—what Paul calls the new creation in 2 Corinthians 5—is made *according to God*! This means he is made in God's likeness. Paul says in Ephesians 4:24

"you put on the new self, the one created according to God's likeness in righteousness and purity of the truth." (HCS)[196]

Paul's words parallel with Genesis. They emphasize the point that the *new creation is as the original creation: wholly of God and **like** God, to further His purposes in the world.* The new man, because it is made in the likeness of God, has the ability to fulfill God's original design. He has made us again to be righteous! With the penalty of sin removed, the weight of our past falls away.

"And to be transformed as you embrace the glorious Christ-within as your new life and live in union with him! For God has re-created you all over again in his perfect righteousness, and you now belong to him in the realm of true holiness." (Ephesians 4:24 TPT)[197]

This gift of re-creation in righteousness transforms us! By living in this union with Him, because He sees us as holy, we aim to bring honor to the life giver. Because we are restored to the righteousness that existed by God's design in Eden, we must put aside the deeds of darkness, and "put on the Lord

Jesus Christ, and make no provision for the flesh in regard to its lusts."[198] We have a new opportunity to experience what He created us for: real communion and partnership with God. But it requires denying our flesh the opportunity to give in to sinful desires.

Examples of the Co-crucified Life of Christ in Us

People of faith throughout history have sought to further God's purposes in the world through what they understood God's unique role for them to be. They knew it could mean giving up comfort and security in favor of hardship, but they were willing to undergo hardship because they, as Paul said in Philippians 3, wanted to know Him better and experience His resurrection power. They wanted their life to reflect the power of Christ through their submission to His will. They adopted the approach of Paul, not considering their lives as dear to themselves.

Growing up, I read many biographies of people who made sacrificial choices to follow Jesus. Corrie Ten Boom, George Mueller, Hudson Taylor, Jim Elliott, and Dietrich Bonhoeffer come to mind. Many people know their names and their stories. Yet there are many others who sacrifice, who die to themselves that Christ may live in them, whose names the world does not know. Yet God knows they have counted their lives valuable to Him by not considering them dear to themselves. David Platt mentions one such woman whom he met in the Himalayan mountains named Maya. She lived and studied in the capital city and became a nurse. She moved to a mountain village that had no medical care even in nearby villages. This meant they had to be well enough to trek a long distance to get qualified care. In making the choice to live there so that people could have medical care closer to these villages, Maya said, "I just want to do what God wants me to do with what God has given me."[199]

Mueller had a similar desire to meet the needs of orphans, trusting God to supply those needs. The number of children who were provided for under his care is astounding. In her classic devotional, L.B. Cowman tells the story of a boat captain who carried Muller onboard to speak in Canada. The captain said,

> "I went to America some years ago with the captain of a steamer, who was a very devoted Christian. When off the coast of Newfoundland he said to me, "The last time I crossed here, five weeks ago, something happened which revolutionized the whole of my Christian life. We had George Mueller of Bristol on board. I had been on the bridge twenty-four hours and never left it. George Mueller came to me, and said, 'Captain I have come to tell you that I must be in Quebec Saturday afternoon.' It is impossible, I said. 'Very well, if your ship cannot take me, God will find some other way. I have never broken an engagement for fifty-seven years. Let us go down into the chart-room and pray.'
>
> I looked at that man of God, and thought to myself, 'What lunatic asylum can that man have come from? I never heard of such a thing as this.' Mr. Mueller, I said, do you know how dense this fog is? 'No,' he replied, 'my eye is not on the density of the fog, but on the living God, who controls every circumstance of my life.' He knelt down and prayed one of the most simple prayers, and when he had finished I was going to pray; but he put his hand on my shoulder, and told me not to pray. 'First, you do not believe He will answer; and second

I BELIEVE HE *HAS*, and there is no need whatever for you to pray about it.' I looked at him, and he said, 'Captain, I have known my Lord for fifty-seven years, and there has never been a single day that I have failed to get audience with the King. Get up, Captain, and open the door, and you will find the fog gone.' I got up, and the fog was indeed gone. On Saturday afternoon, George Mueller was in Quebec for his meeting."[200]

There are several lessons from this episode on the sea. The most evident is that Mueller's approach to the circumstances of his life show he was crucified to self, and this made it possible for him to entreat the King of the Universe to meet his need in service of the gospel. A second truth is that he knew it is not how many pray to God to meet a need, but the basis of their relationship with the Almighty and the certainty of faith to receive the answer. He knew the God he served. He knew that being His son meant he was to ask, and to expect God to act in response to his prayer. The result of asking would be an outcome for his good, as Matthew 7:8–9 says should be our expectation when asking from our Father. He knew God had called him to the work for orphans, and that God had consistently provided their needs. Why would He not meet the need at sea in order that testimony of his work be shared as scheduled?

Mueller's faith moves me. What are the stories of sacrifice and trust in God that move your heart? Maybe it is a missionary or martyr like those I mentioned. Maybe it is someone in your community or among your friends who risks their safety and reputation to serve the needy like Maya in Platt's story. Whoever it may be, the common ingredient is humility. Having denied their old self that served its own needs, they allowed Jesus to come in and live His life through them. They live from the belief that Jesus, who knew no sin, already humbled Himself to the point of death on the cross. Paul, in Philippians 2 and 3, says that when we devote ourselves to working for God's good purposes and pour ourselves out for others we do not labor in vain.[201] Rather, we consider that whatever we have given up in order to live obediently, we view it as trash compared to the value of belonging to Christ.[202] In pursuit of our return to Eden, every sacrificial action is worth it when making Jesus' kingdom known is our goal. For Paul, the key to living "hidden in Him" was to realize that the gift of being a new creation means we become again what we once were, relating to God with the intimacy we were created for. We have this privilege because Jesus became sin for us and took on its penalty, so that the Father could consider us righteous again.[203] This is the blessing of being new creations, and it is really good news.

7

Eden's Promise: Why the Good News is Good

P aul's life was changed forever by knowing the power of Jesus' resurrection and His suffering. He was convinced that God made him righteous by faith and faith alone.[204] Why did he see that as such good news? Why was it different than all he had previously believed? For a zealous Jew, it was radical news that true righteousness was not earned through the law but came instead from God in response to faith. Jesus came to us as heirs of a promise. Paul knew that the gospel he preached emphasized the action of God on our behalf to make us righteous, not on our efforts to become righteous and thus please God. Paul knew that gives us new life and restores the purpose of mankind in God's plan for this world. This gives us high value in God's eyes! Paul believed and taught that God had become man so we could be restored as heirs of a promise, restored to the inheritance promised to Adam and Eve as stewards of His earth.

A few points from earlier chapters on the gospel bear repeating.

➢ Redemption is achieved for us by the work of Jesus on the cross not by a rehabilitation of ourselves. By this redemption, we are made a new creation in which Jesus lives through us.[205]
➢ This new creation is not a product of our righteous deeds. Jesus made this possible because of His faithfulness to

live as the Father directed Him. His obedience resulted in a sinless life that enabled Him to be the "once for all" sacrifice that defeated sin and death. It is not by our good works that we become something new, but by the goodness of the Father, who offers us new life.

➢ Any deeds we do that bring glory to God are because Jesus empowers our life, so we are free from having to earn His pleasure.

This last aspect begins this chapter, to define why that is such good news.

Why Not Having to Earn His Pleasure Is Good News

The fact that our love from God is not based on our goodness is good news because it eliminates the need to be anxious about our struggle with sin. C.S. Lewis shares an analogy that illustrates how our "goodness" is apart from any effort to earn God's pleasure. He says of our natural, earthly body, "A body that is alive is not one that never gets hurt, but one that can to some extent repair itself. In the same way, a Christian is not a man who never does wrong, but a man who is enabled to repent and pick himself up and begin over again after each stumble-because the Christ-life is inside him, repairing him all the time, enabling him to repeat (in some degree) the kind of voluntary death which Christ Himself carried out."[206] Repentance is needed when we stumble. But what a comfort that stumbling does not disqualify us from the life we live in Him.

Also, "that is why the Christian is in a different position from other people who are trying to be good. They hope, by being good, to please God if there is one; or, if they think there is not-at least they hope to deserve approval from good men."[207] We should quit thinking we have to work to please God, because He is already pleased with us when we exercise our faith.[208] A Christian should recognize any good fruit in his life as coming from Christ inside him. Lewis says "God will not love us because we are good, but that God will make us good because He loves us."[209] He loves us, so He empowers us to do His will.

There are very few situations in our world where we are not measured by what we do. In school settings, there are many tests of ability and our performance does define our standing. Then there are evaluations in our jobs as to how well we are achieving the goals set forth by owners or management. Even in human relationships, we can view others based on "what have you done for me lately?" But God's love, and His desire to bring us close to Him again, is different. His great love is expressed living inside us, and it is that indwelling that makes us good! There are so many people still striving, hoping that God may see them as worthy of love. By the measurement the world uses, they hope their good outweighs their bad so they are acceptable to God. But God measures our life by Jesus and His sacrifice. As Paul said, "He made the One who did not know sin to be sin for us, so that we might become the righteousness of God in Him."[210] The point of our faith is not to *behave well* in order to please God, but that we are considered righteous, "made good" before Him because of His love displayed in Christ. How do we view our life once we have become His?

Matthew 20 contains a parable that emphasizes that our gratitude toward God should be for His love and grace in salvation, not based on our sense of fairness. Jesus says the kingdom is like a landowner who went out early in the day to hire workers for his vineyard. Throughout the day, more workers were hired. When the workday was complete, each was paid the same: a full day's wage. The landowner, in response to those grumbling about the equal pay for those who worked less, said, "Don't I have the right to do what I want with my business? Are you jealous because I'm generous?" (Matthew 20:15 HCS)[211] If I look at God as a taskmaster who only wants to get the most out of me, I can become resentful toward others who have served God a shorter time. But if I view Him as a Father who does not offer His love to His children according to how well or how long they served Him, then my response should be gratitude. In other words, we cannot blame others for discovering God's grace later than we did. We should rejoice in our Father's generosity! We have all sinned against our Creator. It would be fair that all men die for sin. None of us deserves what God gives as "wages" for what we do.[212]

The reason the gospel is good news is that God made a way for redemption through Jesus, despite our sin, and despite Adam and Eve's rebellious choice. The truth is that the gospel of Jesus is not about what *I* can do, but what *He has done* to restore me to God. What are the consequences of not rightly teaching the true gospel? The penalty for preaching a false gospel is being cursed! It is that serious. Paul says he can't go back to a law-centered faith, because doing so would rebuild what he once destroyed.[213] It was such good news that Paul would not allow anyone to dilute it, or to deceive people with distortions of it, for doing so carries a heavy consequence in his view.

How is the covenant ushered in by His death different from the covenant based on works? Jesus pays the price for our righteousness; our good works do not. Paul laments fellow Jews who "ignored the righteousness God gives, wanting instead to be acceptable to God because of their own works, they've refused to submit to God's faith-righteousness."[214] The good news is that Jesus brings us into a better covenant, based on better promises than the covenant based on law-keeping.[215]

Paul sees rescue from evil as one of those better promises. Jesus gave Himself up to rescue us from the evil age we are in, and to restore to us all He intended for us in the beginning.[216] Paul knew that rescue was the goal of Jesus' coming. He equates the results of rescue to a transfer of domains, to coming under a new authority. Rescue is central to the gospel, as Paul says: "For He rescued us from the domain of darkness, and transferred us to the kingdom of His beloved Son.[217] He removed us from living under the dark rule of the god of the world, and moved us into Jesus' kingdom. And He didn't just transfer us, He was pleased to—He longed to do it![218]

As a new creation under this new authority, we operate with new power against our enemy. Being out from under Satan's domain frees us to operate in God's plan and purpose. A domain is a place where authority is clearly defined. If we speak about our house as a domain, we mean that we are in charge in that place. We own the house, so we have authority over it. When we were under darkness, our enemy Satan dominated our thinking. Paul says before He rescued us, we were under "the god of this world."[219] The reason Satan is called ruler, or god, of this world is that our original sin gave him the authority over the earth that was ours by God's design. But when we get rescued, instead of being captive to the authority of Satan who rebelled against God, we now belong to Jesus' kingdom! By his perfect obedience to the Father's will while on earth, He gives us power to take back our authority from our enemy by living out God's purpose. By fulfilling the works what He prepared for us to do, we bring His kingdom's influence to earth, and aid in His will being done on earth as it is in heaven![220]

The Good News of Rescue Changes Us

How can we tell from Paul's life that he was convinced of the "goodness" of the message he proclaimed? One evidence is found where he describes his *new life* in Jesus. Paul said he had found the secret of having plenty and at other times, being in want.[221] He was not swayed by either financial surplus or need, whether "having much or having little." That sounds like a man who was "rescued" from an evil age because most people in this age can't get enough things, enough "likes," or enough pleasure. And therefore they consider themselves in want. Life requires us to pay for what we need, but Paul knew that God meets our needs. That confidence freed him from worry over provision. That is fruit of the good news of the faithful character of His Father.

Second, Paul says concerning his earthly life that "to live is Christ and to die is gain."[222] Either way, whether he stayed on earth for "their sakes" or he died and was then present with Jesus, Paul knew he "won." Paul was hard pressed over this question. He wanted to be with Jesus, but he knew he would remain on earth as it was necessary for other people's sake. He believed God was not finished with him, that all God had marked out for him to do had not yet been accomplished. He knew that if he remained on earth, through the Spirit, he could do all things through Jesus who strengthened him.[223] By ourselves, we can't handle the weight of His glorious purpose He designed us for or for difficult circumstances that may come. Paul said to Timothy that "all who desire to live a godly life in Christ Jesus will be persecuted." (2 Timothy 3:12 ESV)[224] But if we agree with Paul that, if we live, we have Jesus' power and presence, and that if we die, it is gain, then we can handle any outcome. If neither death nor life can separate us from His love, that is good news![225]

Appreciating Good News

How do you react to good news? With skepticism? With "why do I deserve this?" With a loud shout that "it's about time!" I'd like to think I react with excitement. The truth is many people are used to experiencing more bad than good news. Because bad news can cause emotions that discourage us, receiving good news, while exciting, may just bring a sense of relief that the news is not worse. Maybe your relief is that your child endured a difficult season of relationships and came out the other side strong or had a difficult year in school yet they performed better than expected.

I have experienced tough news numerous times over the last five years. The response of "relief" came when the surgeon said about cancerous masses, "We believe we got it all." I have experienced this multiple times with my wife and other immediate family members. While very thankful for detection and the results of surgery, as well as continued healthy life, dealing with circumstances you hope to never face affects us. One result of facing hardship is that "bad" news conditions us to protect our heart from all news. It takes the shine off good news if we only treat that news with relief instead of the joy it deserves.

But the reality of the news God gives—that we are made for Eden, made for a valuable role in His plans, and empowered to fulfill our role—should bring joy when we really grasp what God is offering. This "good news" is more than just a balancing out of the "good" and "bad" news we get in life, which keeps us neither too excited nor too down. The good news in Jesus is more meaningful than healing from an illness or mending of a friendship. It is the gift of something we cannot repay. The future which we are given, and the alternative from which we are spared, is so wonderful that no bad news can counter-balance it. There is nothing of equal weight that can make this good news "lesser" than the sum of all our hopes. We cannot just accept it and "move on." It is the great news that no earthly situation can negate or dim. The contrast between this news and any other good news you may receive is worthy of some elaboration.

The Gospel Is Good News When You Know Its Full Scope

To understand how "good" the message is, we must avoid limiting the gospel's scope. The first way we might limit it is to misjudge our condition before we came to God. Jesus did not come and die to make bad people into good people. He came to bring life to people who were spiritually dead.

God "made us alive with the Messiah even though we were dead in trespasses. You are saved by grace!" (Ephesians 2:5 HCS)[226]

> "And when you were dead in trespasses and in the uncircumcision of your flesh, *He made you alive with Him and forgave us all our trespasses.*" (Colossians 2:13 HCS) [227] (italics mine)

Paul says both are true. We did receive forgiveness of sin, but the fact that sin made us dead people, not just bad people, means that we had to be made alive so we could receive the benefit of not being slaves to sin any longer.

This distinction is essential because many believers have been taught that the gospel means a reprieve from hell and forgiveness of sin. This is a second way we may limit the message, by focusing on heaven or hell instead of redemption. The rest of the gospel, the fact that because we were made alive and now have His life, God's empowerment,

116

flowing through us, may get pushed to the background. This view limits the message of the gospel to our need to embrace forgiveness for salvation. There are several dangers to this viewpoint. One danger comes from assuming that once we become part of God's family by accepting that forgiveness, we are "good to go." That is, inclusion in His family should provide enough knowledge of the truth for us to overcome the temptations of this present life until He returns to take us all home. In other words, once we have our "ticket" into heaven, we steadily coast toward the day we die. But just knowing that as His child His power is available to us will not produce the fruitful life as a new creation that Paul describes. We must humble ourselves by thinking of our life as not our own. Then like Paul, we "win" whether we remain on the earth or enter eternity. Our purpose while on earth is vital to the redemption of people and of creation. We know heaven awaits us. But fulfilling our earthly purpose reflects that we understand how good the gospel is.

The gospel is good news because we don't have to depend on the quality or quantity of our works in order to spend eternity with Him as citizens of His kingdom. Rather, we serve in His kingdom because Jesus loved us enough to die for our sin. Instead of relying on our deeds, we walk in the good works He prepared beforehand for us.[228] What He created us to accomplish for Him was defined before we ever took a breath. And in fulfilling the works He assigned to us, we can "please Him in all respects, bearing fruit in every good work and increasing in the knowledge of God"[229] It's far easier to gratefully serve Him when we realize our Creator has already prepared in advance everything He hopes our lives will become. This lifts the burden from us of trying to do enough to bring something of worth to Him.

We can then spend our precious time striving to do more of the actions He set out for us, and engage in the relationships

He prepared for us, rather than expending effort trying to compare ourselves with someone else's "workmanship." He has called us each to be a different expression of His creativity, as He makes each of us unique, fitted for the calling He has on our life. I don't need to imitate the works He has called others to; I need to discover what He prepared ahead for me! The truth about a work of art is that its creator knows fully what he intends it to mean or to reflect for those who see it. A written work, like a poem, expresses an author's intent.[230] God's intent for us, says Paul, was to make us alive when we were dead. We couldn't earn it, but because He is rich in mercy and so that He could show us His rich grace forever, He gave us a gift. A timely gift, to show us truths that could only be understood after Jesus came to earth.

The Gift of Good News as a Mystery Revealed

The gospel is good news because it doesn't focus on our attempts to make our lives worthy of rescue, but on God, who rescued us, knowing we could not escape Satan's dark domain and enter into God's kingdom without help. That required the sacrifice of Jesus, so that not only are we forgiven, but we enter into works He prepared for us to do before we were even restored to relationship with Him. Jesus gave us a gift by dying so that He might live through us. A gift that would restore us to what He meant for us before sin entered Eden. This gift is a life with God living *in* us and *with* us! It's a life of hope, empowered by the promises of God. We are of God's household, His sons, His daughters, His very own.

This gift is the essence of the "mystery" that Paul says is brought to the attention of the heavenly realm through the Church. Paul sees the gospel as evidence—to both the righteous and fallen spirits—of the purpose which the Father fulfills in Jesus.[231] He is in Jesus fulfilling the promise of redeeming our purpose. This mystery was not known to previous generations of people. But we are given intimate knowledge of His plans! We live after Jesus was revealed as the crown of God's work to redeem men. How could we not have the outlook of Paul if we see the gospel as the culmination of what God had been doing from the time of Eden?[232] God demonstrated His nature in Jesus in a way that had never been known. What was being accomplished for mankind in Jesus was a new demonstration of His plan to restore us to Eden. We have been told what was hidden for many centuries.

Seeing the Gospel as Good News Affects Our Outlook on Life

When taught in its fullness, the gospel is truly good news. And when we acknowledge that our life is not our own, we are rooted and grounded in the love of God, to whom our life belongs. Who lived with such an awareness that His life was not His own? Jesus did! John quotes Jesus:

> "I am the good shepherd. The good shepherd lays down his life for the sheep
> …and I lay down My life for the sheep."[233]

> "This is why the Father loves Me, because I am laying down My life so I may take it up again. No one takes it from Me, but I lay it down on My own." (John 10:17-18 HCS)[234]

> "When Jesus had received the sour wine, He said, 'It is finished!' Then bowing His head, He gave up His spirit." (John 19:30 HCS) [235]

The Apostle John saw that Jesus considered His life not as His own, but as serving the purpose of the Father to show us His love. "No one has greater love than this, that someone would lay down his life for his friends." (John 15:13 HCS) [236] And "This is how we have come to know love: He laid down His life for us." (1 John 3:16 HCS) [237]

Jesus did not die because a Roman leader sentenced him to death. He laid down His life for the sheep who would belong to the Father. He was slain for men long before He appeared in front of Pilate.[238] With the plan for Jesus determined ahead of our sin, we can marvel at the plan for us, as David did in Psalm 139, knowing that our days are ordained.[239]

Jesus gave His life for us, and that is great news. But He also modeled for us how to live. He displayed all the fruits of the spirit. Since that was true of Jesus, what are the results of following His message and imitating Him? Another way to ask this is, "What is the Gospel supposed to do to a person? What is the effect of embracing good news?" Perhaps in answering that, we can see examples from Jesus' life, how living by God's direction affected His earthly relationships for the good of others. What do we show others about God when we follow Jesus? What do we reflect to them concerning Christlikeness? Why would they want the kind of life Jesus lives inside a believer?

Living with confidence in the good news produces a knowledge of how the Father would respond to the unexpected. Do you recall the wedding in Cana when Jesus showed up and produced an unexpected outcome? John 2 is a very telling account of how Jesus' confidence in His message and identity from His Father gave Him the ability to bless others in circumstances where they had nowhere to turn. Turning water to wine goes against the way and the timing in which we might have expected Jesus to reveal Himself. A healing miracle comes to mind as an ideal first revelation of

His identity. But as a picture of the future wedding feast He will celebrate with His bride the Church and to honor his mother's faith, Jesus turned water into wine. Jesus made the wine great, better than the wine that ran out! The servant in John 2 said the usual practice at a wedding is to serve lesser quality wine at the end once guests have partaken freely. But he said this groom has saved the excellent, the best, for last![240] Jesus knew the miracle would glorify His Father and witness to those present His miracle-working nature. He provided a blessing for a groom. But more than this gift to the host of the wedding, and to the witnesses of a miracle, Jesus was looking ahead to the future kingdom. In providing this wine miraculously, He prefigured His future celebration with wine alongside His redeemed after His return. Jesus told His disciples, "I tell you, from this moment I will not drink of this fruit of the vine until that day when I drink it in a new way in My Father's kingdom with you." (Matthew 26:29 HCS) [241] This same Jesus, who demonstrated power over the natural in that miracle, lives inside us. That is good news!

Jesus lived with assurance that the gospel is good news. This assurance is reflected in His invitation to come to Him for rest. Jesus says, "Come to Me, all who are weary and heavy-laden, and I will give you rest. Take my yoke upon you and learn from me, for I am gentle and humble in heart. my yoke is easy and my burden light." (Matthew 11:28-30 NAS 1995) [242] Life here can be hard, but learning how to walk as He walked, in humility, gives rest instead of weariness. The good works He has for us are not a burden. That makes His invitation to come to Him good news. Jesus knows that trying to live our life without the plan that He ushered in—to indwell us and to create a new man—would wear us out. He knows that only His way offers true rest. When we live apart from the Father, we are subject to straying, more likely to sin, and prone to be limited in our effectiveness as His workmanship.

What relief would come to our lives if we would live by His empowerment and walk in the kind of closeness Jesus had with the Father! That would give us confidence and peace to make decisions that will honor Him.

How the Good News Helps Us Grow in Christ

Paul expresses the glory of a life transformed by the promise of the good news. The result of this transformation is that our life looks more like Jesus! And by looking more like Him, we bring Him glory. In 2 Corinthians 3:18, Paul says:

"Nothing between us and God, our faces shining with the brightness of his face. And so we are transfigured much like the Messiah, our lives gradually becoming brighter and more beautiful as God enters our lives and we become like him." (MSG)[243]

Or alternately, "We can all draw close to him with the veil removed from our faces. And with no veil we all become like mirrors who brightly reflect the glory of the Lord *Jesus*. We are being transfigured into his very image as we move from one brighter level of glory to another. And this glorious transfiguration comes from the Lord, who is the Spirit." (2 Corinthians 3:18 TPT).[244] We were created in His image, and when we know His true nature, His glory, we grow into what we were created to be: image-bearers. For our lives to brightly reflect the glory of the Lord Jesus, we must see the goodness in the message that we are "Made for Eden" and are therefore being transformed by His power.

Peter describes how to best prepare ourselves for His return, by adding to our faith.

"Everything we could ever need for life and complete devotion to God has already been deposited in us by His divine power. *For all this was lavished upon us* through the rich experience of knowing Him who has called us by name and invited us to come to Him through a glorious manifestation of His goodness. As a result of this, He has given you magnificent promises that are beyond all price, so that through *the power of* these tremendous promises you can experience partnership with the divine nature, by which you have escaped the corrupt desires that are of the world.

So devote yourselves to lavishly supplementing your faith with goodness, and to goodness add understanding, and to understanding add the strength of self-control, and to self-control add patient endurance, and to patient endurance add godliness, and to godliness add mercy toward your brothers and sisters, and to mercy toward others add unending love.

Since these virtues are already *planted* deep within, and you possess them in abundant supply, they will keep you from being inactive or fruitless in your pursuit of knowing Jesus Christ more intimately. But if anyone lacks these things, he is blind, constantly closing his eyes to the mysteries of our faith, and forgetting *his innocence*—for his past sins have been washed away. For this reason, beloved ones, be eager to confirm and validate that God has invited you *to salvation* and claimed you as His own. If you do these things, you will never stumble." 2 Peter 1:3-10 (TPT).[245]

Peters says these virtues are ours in abundant supply. His power has deposited into us what is necessary for us to serve Him! The fact that He saved us is a display of His goodness. Out of His complete goodness, He gave us magnificent promises by which we can experience partnership with Him, through the divine nature He put inside when He made us new creations. And through our partnership in the divine with Him, we have escaped the corrupt desires that are of the world. Paul said we are no longer obligated to live according to the flesh. We've been given new power through a new presence inside us, and this presence frees us from having to follow the world's evil desires.

Peter says we are to devote ourselves to adding traits to our faith, and the result of this process is that we won't stumble! In other words, as we devote ourselves to becoming like Him by having self-control, patience, and love for our brothers, we will not fail! When we add these qualities to our life, they keep us from being unfruitful. They keep us useful to the Master and fruitful in serving Him. The Word of God trains us into useful service to Him.[246] Now that's good news! If we have those characteristics added to our faith continually, to keep us effective and useful, we accept an unparalleled offer from God for resources to be given to us for living as He designed us to.

How We Exercise Our Belief that the Gospel is Good

Once we are convinced that the gospel really is good news, we must not go backward. We should not lose passion for being living examples of His grace. Paul ends this chapter of 2 Corinthians by saying that as a result of his perspective on his trials, and the death of Jesus for us, he does not give up or lose heart. He keeps planting seeds of the goodness of the message.

> "Therefore we do not lose heart, but though our outer man is decaying, yet our inner man is being renewed day by day. For momentary, light affliction is producing for us an eternal weight of glory far beyond all comparison, while we look not at the things which are seen, but at the things which are not seen; for the things which are seen are temporal, but the things which are not seen are eternal." (2 Corinthians 4:16-18 NAS 1995)[247]

We show that we understand the gospel to be good news when we view every hardship on this earth as temporary. What we see will fade away. When we embrace the eternal, which we can't see, this perspective helps us view the hardship rightly. We can then live with joy despite challenging situations.

Therefore, knowing why the good news is so good changes how we respond to trials, affects how we persevere in the transformation process God has us in, and helps us realize the joy our lives are meant for. It also enables us to move into the "good works" God prepared for us beforehand.

But knowing the gospel is good news is not the only key to fostering the Eden life Paul shows us in Galatians 2:20. We must know how Jesus and Paul describe the various identities of our new life in God are expressed, and how we are to live according to those identities in our restoration to God's original purpose. We must realize we are stewards, but even greater, we are sons who can walk in freedom as we follow Him.

8

Reflections of Eden: Freedom and Sonship

The message of Jesus living His life through us is *really* good news. That good news demonstrates that what God began in Eden reaches its highest point in the promises of the New Covenant of new life. These promises are made to those who believe. One of those benefits of the promised new life is freedom. Can you remember moments when the truth that the gospel is good news made you feel totally free?

An experience I had with some friends backpacking in Glacier National Park in Montana produced this feeling. We had a campsite near Glenns Lake, where the water is so clear you can see the mountain peaks behind the lake reflecting on the surface, and see down to the beautiful stones made smooth and round by water and time, lining the lake bottom. We had just set up our tents when several deer entered the site and began grazing. Even though we watched them intently, they were not afraid of our presence. Moments later, wading into the lake's edge with sore feet, I welcomed the feeling of relief the cold water brought. In the twilight of the day, looking across the lake at jagged, snow-traced peaks just beyond the water's edge, that evening was one of several moments that week that caused me to give thanks for God's creativity and beauty. But the reason that seeing the beauty of deer, glacial lakes, and towering peaks felt so freeing is that I was enjoying my Father's world. In that moment, I was free to enjoy the place we had traveled all day to reach. A rugged trail gave way to enjoyment of the gift. This beauty gave me a glimpse of the freedom I was made for. It touched the place within me that C.S. Lewis spoke of, the desire for the other world that I was made for, that can truly satisfy the desire for beauty and perfection.

What I felt in Montana was freedom. But *that* freedom only lasted for those moments. All too quickly, I was whisked away from the beauty, and back to the matrix of life. But what Jesus intended to give us is lasting freedom, freedom from sin and death. When we walk in His freedom, we can experience the other gift He promised: sonship. Living with our return to Eden in view requires finding the freedom that reconciliation with God provides.

Freedom as a Reflection of Eden life

We've seen in earlier chapters that being new creations in Jesus frees us from death. Paul says that freedom is what Jesus intended us to gain by His death and resurrection. "It was for freedom that Christ set us free; therefore keep standing firm and do not be subject again to a yoke of slavery."[248] Paul was adamant that once we have been set free to serve Jesus, we must not turn back to what enslaved us! This is because Jesus is the source of *true* freedom. "So if the Son sets you free, you really will be free."[249] True freedom is not permission to do whatever makes us happy, regardless of if it is contrary to God's best. But true freedom is an opportunity to serve Jesus out of a conviction of who He is: the true King and Redeemer of all. "Act as free men, and do not use your freedom as a covering for evil, but use it as bondslaves of God." (1 Peter 2:16 NAS 1995)[250] In other words, being free is not a reason to do what our flesh wants but is an invitation to follow the One who set us free! You show you have accepted that invitation and are free from your old self and its master Satan when you consistently refuse to love the world. By not loving the world, we instead focus on and prioritize the things our Father has set before us to do. And in doing them, we live out His will and please Him. I took pleasure from being in God's beautiful creation in Montana, where I felt His presence through what He made. I believe we please Him when we enjoy His creation and the feeling of freedom that produces.

Journey to Freedom: Israel's Slavery

The nation of Israel experienced slavery during their time in Egypt. Joseph was betrayed by his brothers and sold into slavery there. Years later, after Joseph prospered there in service to the Pharaoh, his brothers came to Egypt to avoid famine. Their hardship began when a different leader of Egypt arose. Exodus 1 says, "a new king, who had not known Joseph, came to power in Egypt." (Exodus 1:8 HCS)[251] That king, out of fear of Israel's size and power if they turned against Egypt, forced them into hard labor. We learn that God raised up a deliverer in Moses, and in a series of miraculous plagues, God judged Egypt's Pharaoh for his treatment of Israel. God said He would bring His people out of Egypt by the judgments He brought upon the Egyptians.[252] Though Israel was delivered from the hand of Pharaoh, they were unable to find real freedom for another generation. Because those spying out the land failed to believe God would empower them to conquer the giants there, the Israelites wandered for forty years. God promised Abraham land as Israel's inheritance. God also promised Abraham that he would become father of, and a blessing to, many nations. God even changed his name from Abram to Abraham as a sign of these promises.

Two of the most amazing chapters in the Bible describe a pivotal moment in Israel's history. In these chapters, we witness how slavery in Egypt affected the thinking of the Israelite leaders, which then hindered them from acting on God's promise. In Numbers 13 and 14, we see the result of spying in the land of Canaan, which God commanded them to do. After scouting the land for forty days, they return to Moses with its fruit. They agreed with the description God had promised for the land.[253] "It certainly does flow with milk and honey, and this is its fruit."[254] That sounds like Eden, a land of plenty and blessing. But the spies said, "However, the people living in the land are strong and the cities large and fortified." (Numbers 13:28 HCS) [255] Perhaps they doubted that God would really come through for them, and instead let intimidation rule their minds. Despite Caleb's challenge to the others that "we must go up and take possession of the land because we can certainly conquer it," the majority said they couldn't do so because the people were stronger than they were. (Numbers 13:30 HCS) [256] So they made claims about the land that were contrary to God's description. "The land we passed through to explore is one that devours its inhabitants." (Numbers 13:32 HCS) [257] The Israelites didn't see God's presence with them, and the provisions for their well-being, that God intended for them as they overcame the enemy. They failed to remember how He made His presence and provision available in Eden to Adam and Eve. He walked with them often, and He gave them everything they needed to thrive in Eden. The ten spies didn't believe the provision God demonstrated in Eden was available to them in that moment, but instead focused on their own abilities, and believed they were not up to the task God called them to fulfill, taking the land of promise. They said, "We were like grasshoppers in our own sight, and so we were in their sight."[258]

These words brought weeping, complaining, and doubting among Israel. The Israelites questioned God's good nature, asking why God would bring them out of Egypt only to let them die by the sword in Canaan. "Would it not be better for us to return to Egypt?"[259] Egypt represented slavery and hardship, so their desire to return shows they were still thinking like slaves! Saying that slavery was better than death in the land shows a total distrust of God's promise. He promised them their own land, where they would be free to enjoy His provision. Once more, because of their confidence in the promise, Joshua and Caleb attempted to convince fellow Israelites that God would move on their behalf, just as He said He would.

> "The land we passed through and explored is an extremely good land. If the LORD is pleased with us, He will bring us into this land, a land flowing with milk and honey, and give it to us. Only don't rebel against the LORD, and don't be afraid of the people of the land, for we will devour them." (Numbers 14:7-9 HCS)[260]

Their fellow Israelites wanted to stone them for disagreeing with the consensus on the impossibility of the task. God asked Moses, "How long will they not trust in Me despite all the signs I have performed among them?" (Numbers 14:11 HCS)[261] Moses pleaded with God not to destroy Israel, and God said, "I have pardoned them as you requested. Yet as surely as I live and as the whole earth is filled with the LORD's glory, none of the men who have seen My glory and the signs I performed in Egypt and in the wilderness, and have tested Me these ten times and did not obey Me, will ever see the land I swore to give their fathers. None of those who have despised Me will see it." (Numbers 14:20-23 HCS)[262] Yet God says a different future exists for Caleb due to his faith in God which produced obedience. "But since My servant Caleb has a different spirit and has followed Me completely, I will bring him into the land where he has gone, and his descendants will inherit it." (Numbers 14:24 HCS)[263] God also told Moses that for the Israelites failing to enter the land, His actions toward them would be exactly as the words they spoke. "Tell them: As surely as I live," this is the Lord's declaration, "I will do to you exactly as I heard you say." (Numbers 14:28 HCS)[264] Men's words, because they are spoken by stewards of creation, carry power. Remember that the name Adam gave to the animals is what their name became.[265] Whether speaking life or death, words continue to be powerful after Adam and Eve's sin. Life and death are in the power of the tongue.[266] Caleb's and Joshua's words about the promised land being plentiful, and the Israelites' ability through God to conquer it, were a powerful witness to God's promise, and held authority before God the covenant keeper. From God's viewpoint, it would be according to their words, and thus, according to their faith. The majority of the spies who argued that the land could not be taken, were victims of their own thinking. Only Caleb and Joshua, who believed God would fulfill His promise of land for His people and would enable them to conquer that land, would enter. In His mercy, God would allow the descendants of the remaining spies to conquer the land, but the spies' unbelieving words prevented them from conquering its inhabitants.

The Israelites wanted freedom, but when they took their eyes off the promise and instead focused on the giants in the land, they failed. We also want freedom, but if we don't trust that God has set us free from sin and death, we, too, will miss the blessing. The book of Deuteronomy is full of God's promises to Israel for blessing in the promised land if they would follow what He taught them. Israel's future entry to that land is accomplished by Joshua. But prior to Israel's entry, Moses tells the people what they should tell their children about the freedom the land represents.

"When the LORD your God brings you into the land He swore to your fathers Abraham, Isaac, and Jacob that He would give you-a land with large and beautiful cities that you did not build, houses full of every good thing that you did not fill them with, wells dug that you did not dig, and vineyards and olive groves that you did not plant-and when you eat and are satisfied, be careful not to forget the LORD who brought you out of the land of Egypt, out of the place of slavery." (Deuteronomy 6:10-12 HCS)[267]

"When your son asks you in the future, 'What is the meaning of the decrees, statutes, and ordinances, which the LORD our God has commanded you?' tell him, 'We were slaves of Pharaoh in Egypt, but the LORD brought us out of Egypt with a strong hand. Before our eyes the LORD inflicted great and devastating signs and wonders on Egypt, on Pharaoh, and on all his household, but He brought us from there in order to lead us in and give us the land that He swore to our fathers. The LORD commanded us to follow all these statutes and to fear the LORD our God for our prosperity always and for our preservation, as it is today. Righteousness will be ours if we are careful to follow every one of these commands before the LORD our God, as He has commanded us.'" (Deuteronomy 6:20-25 HCS)[268]

Moses knew they would be tempted to forget God, who had brought them out of their slavery in Egypt, then gave them the land and its abundant blessings. Over time, Israel would violate God's commands, yet God was faithful to His people and preserved them. In an honest, repentant prayer, Ezra says, "Though we are slaves, our God has not abandoned us in our slavery...He has extended grace to us...giving us new life" (Ezra 9:9 HCS)[269] Nehemiah also admits, "Here we are today, slaves in the land You gave our ancestors so that they could enjoy its fruit and its goodness." (Nehemiah 9:36 HCS)[270] He said God gave the land so that they could enjoy its goodness, but "its abundant produce is for the kings whom you have set over us, because of our sins."[271]

Israel experienced slavery because of their many failures to follow God's ways. Yet through His prophets, God promised them that a deliverer was coming. He repeated the promise often, especially in Isaiah, as a way out of the slavery that sin produces. And the deliverer did eventually arrive. He was God's Son, Jesus. The announcement of His name at His birth was the statement of His identity and purpose. "She will give birth to a son, and you are to name Him Jesus, because He will save His people from their sins." (Matthew 1:21 HCS)[272] Luke says Jesus began teaching in the synagogues in Galilee; and in Nazareth, when the scroll of Isaiah is given to Him, He reads from it concerning His purpose and freedom.

> "The scroll of the prophet Isaiah was given to Him, and unrolling the scroll, He found the place where it was written: 'The Spirit of the Lord is on Me, because He has anointed Me to preach good news to the poor. He has sent Me to proclaim freedom to the captives and recovery of sight to the blind, to set free the oppressed, to proclaim the year of the Lord's favor.'" (Luke 4:17-19 HCS)[273]

Luke says He read, gave the scroll back, and sat down. "And the eyes of everyone in the synagogue were fixed on Him. He began by saying to them, 'Today as you listen, this

Scripture has been fulfilled.'" (Luke 4:20-21 HCS) [274] Jesus began His ministry by stating the Father sent Him to proclaim freedom! God brought freedom from the slavery that Israel had experienced in their past. He won our freedom from slavery to the sin that Adam and Eve brought on mankind. There is the incredible tie-in. As He is proclaiming in the book of Luke what He came to bring us, Jesus is thinking of the freedom that was lost in Genesis and of Israel in Egypt! The bondage that held Adam and Eve in shame and afflicted Israel in Egypt is now overcome in Jesus. The good news is that Jesus makes us truly free from our past. It's no longer a question of how to get free; Jesus accomplishes it for us! "So if the Son sets you free from sin, then become a true son and be unquestionably free!" (John 8:36 TPT)[275]

The Impact of the Cross on Freedom

Years after Jesus' death, the apostle Paul enters. He is a devout Jew who understood the slavery, both literal and spiritual, in Israel's history. In his letter to Rome, over the course of four chapters he explains the relationship of sin, death, and new life. He shows the differences between Adam and Jesus and demonstrates why those who receive Jesus' life into their own are free.

Paul says we were reconciled to God while we were His enemies, because Christ chose to die for sinners. We needed to be reconciled to God because spiritual death is the result of Adam's sin.

"Therefore, just as sin entered the world through one man, and death through sin, in this way death spread to all men, because all sinned…Since by the one man's trespass, death reigned through that one man, how much more will those who receive the overflow of grace and the gift of righteousness reign in life through the one man, Jesus Christ. So then, as through one trespass there is condemnation for everyone, so also through one righteous act there is life-giving justification for everyone." (Romans 5:12, 17-18 HCS)[276]

We all received death as the consequence of Adam's sin. By Jesus' sacrifice, grace results in eternal life.[277] In Romans 7, we see Paul's struggle with a flesh that cannot obey God as his mind wishes. After his description of the struggle within, Paul arrives at a question. "Who will set me free from this body? Jesus will!" Paul said, "for we know that our old self was crucified with Him in order that sin's dominion over the body may be abolished, so that we may no longer be enslaved to sin, since a person who has died is freed from sin's claims." (Romans 6:6-7 HCS)[278] Jesus sacrificed Himself to abolish the power of sin over us, and Paul says when we are crucified with Him, we are freed![279]

It should humble us to think that we became free at the cost of Jesus' life. But that is how much He loves us. His death brings us life because we are free from what held us in bondage. Paul uses the example of marriage earlier in Romans 7 to illustrate death bringing freedom. When a spouse dies, the living spouse is no longer "bound" to them. So it is when we die to sin. We are no longer bound to it. Instead, we are bound to righteousness, and to God as Master.[280]

Understanding Real Freedom, Walking in Sonship

Many believers want to live with freedom but do not do so. The apostle Paul showed us freedom depends on walking in our sonship. We aren't fully free if we expect to be abandoned by God, to experience lack, or if we expect punishment for not living as we should. Sonship means that we belong, that we have access to all that we need, and that we are under no condemnation. Paul describes the link between freedom and sonship in Romans.

The idea of being a "son" is not a gender-bound topic. I will, as Scripture does, use the term to describe being heirs to the promises of God. To become an heir of God is of course offered and intended for both male and female, son and daughter. The "adoption as sons" Paul teaches is an identity not tied to gender. In embracing the victory of His death and resurrection, we are born again as God's children; we become sons and daughters by entering into our inheritance called sonship, the adoption as sons.[281]

Paul says that when we were adopted, we received a spirit of being "brought in." The term is most always translated "adoption." We take that to mean he who was not a child of the family is now a child. Contrary to some individuals' faulty views of adoption—that one who is adopted is less worthy than a "natural born" child to receive the inheritance—the term does not distinguish between natural and adopted. In the Greek, the meaning of the word is "to make a son." The combination of two words, it means to set or place as a son. It's not a question of worth. It's a question of position. All who are made sons receive the promised inheritance. All who belong to God were once far from Him, then were brought near by Jesus' sacrifice, and they became sons.[282] All who are reconciled to God are adopted, born again as His very own.[283] Paul says, "But you have received the 'Spirit of full acceptance,' enfolding you into the family of God. And you will never feel orphaned, for as he rises up within us, our spirits join him in saying the words of tender affection, 'Beloved Father!'" (Romans 8:15 TPT)[284] Our entry into His family was not by chance, for by it He becomes our Father, and He accepts us as His beloved children. "Having predestined us to adoption as sons by Jesus Christ to Himself, according to the good pleasure of His will, to the praise of the glory of His grace, by which He made us accepted in the Beloved."(Ephesians 1:5-6 NKJV)[285]

Romans 7 reminds us how we were freed from sin and death. In Romans 8, Paul links freedom and sonship. This chapter describes the freedom that sons of God are meant for. A life of sonship is led by the Holy Spirit.

Some of the key verses are:

Romans 8:1–2 "Therefore, no condemnation now exists for those in Christ Jesus, because the Spirit's law of life in Christ Jesus has set you free from the law of sin and of death." (NAS 1995)[286]

Romans 8:15 "For you have not received a spirit of slavery leading to fear again, but you have received a spirit of adoption as sons by which we cry out, 'Abba! Father!'" (NAS 1995)[287]

Romans 8:21 "that the creation itself will also be set free from the bondage of corruption into the glorious freedom of God's children." (HCS)[288]

Romans 8:23 "And not only this, but also we ourselves, having the first fruits of the Spirit, even we ourselves groan within ourselves, waiting eagerly for *our* adoption as sons, the redemption of our body." (NAS 1995)[289]

Paul believes that sonship is the reward of our redemption from sin and our resulting reconciliation with Him. This is really good news! Not only are we free, but we are family!

Paul says God sent Jesus "so that He might redeem those who were under the Law, that we might receive the adoption as sons." (Galatians 4:5 NAS 1995)[290] Paul says "He (God) predestined us to adoption as sons through Jesus Christ to Himself, according to the kind intention of His will ..." (Ephesians 1:5 NAS 1995)[291] Finally, Paul shows in Romans 8:21 that the final fruit of our adoption is in the future. Our bodies will be redeemed to match the perfection of our spirit, which was already achieved at our salvation. This redemption is part of the return to the Eden life we are promised. It's the future hope of returning to the life that God made for His sons and daughters. We get back a life as His own people, as it was in Eden and with Israel! This is so encouraging to me and gets me excited for the future.

Sonship in the Gospels

In Luke 15, we see a parable that gives us the same story of rebellion versus obedience, the story of the Prodigal Son. It shows us the heart of the Father. We see the younger son's desire for more of his share of the estate and his fear of missing out. He gathered everything, went on a journey, and squandered his money through loose living. Yet the younger son's fear of hunger takes over after the money is spent. The parable says, "and he would have gladly filled his stomach with the pods that the swine were eating, and no one was giving anything to him." (Luke 15:16 NAS 1995)[292] He also feared having *forfeited* his *identity* as a son. He rehearsed a speech which he would say to his Father, "I am no longer worthy to be called your son; make me as one of your hired men." (Luke 15:19 NAS 1995)[293] Really, he feared disappointing his Father so badly that the position he had reached might have been one from which he couldn't recover. He was feeling shame over his choices and his plight. He realized he might not be considered a son anymore, but He knew His father to be a good man who fed his servants. Here he was hungry, but he was son of a father who fed those under his charge.

He gave a humble speech to the Father. "Father, I have sinned against heaven and in your sight. I'm no longer worthy to be called your son."[294] As the son spoke, his Father placed on him the signs of sonship—the ring and the robe—and demonstrated that sonship wasn't lost. His identity as a son was not nullified by him squandering the estate. The father is clearly a picture of our God, who always desires a restored relationship over judgment. The point of the parable is that "this son of mine was dead and is alive again; he was lost and is found!" (Luke 15:24 HCS)[295] The application of the parable is that separation from the Father is death. Restoration to the Father brings life! When we are restored to the Father, and know the permanency of our sonship with Him, we are fully alive, and are truly free. We believe in His goodness, displayed by His readiness to receive us back when we wander. God's goodness draws people to return to Him, as did the son in the parable who "came to his senses." As He has always been with His people, He is waiting only for the return of His own, in a posture of repentance, so that restoration can occur.

Sonship in Other Letters of Paul

Romans isn't the only place we see that we are God's family in our current and future life with God. Paul reinforces the theme of Romans 6–8 in his letter to the Galatians. He says, "For as many of you as have been baptized into Christ have put on Christ like a garment ... And if you belong to Christ, then you are Abraham's seed, heirs according to the promise." (Galatians 3:27-29 HCS)[296] If you have died with Christ, you have put Jesus on, like a garment. You are an heir to the promise made to Abraham, having a direct line to Christ as His own.

Paul says that adoption means we are sons, heirs of Abraham and of the promise.

"When the time came to completion, God sent His Son, born of a woman, born under the law, to redeem those under the law, so that we might receive adoption as sons. And because you are sons, God has sent the Spirit of His Son into our hearts, crying, "*Abba*, Father!" So you are no longer a slave but a son, and if a son, then an heir through God." (Galatians 4:4-7 HCS)[297]

Paul also says God predestined us to adoption as sons through Jesus Christ.[298] We work so hard in our natural lives to gain freedom, but Christ willingly gave it to us. If we belong to Him, freedom is ours. Why do we have a hard time accepting it and instead try to work for it? How long has mankind struggled to understand sonship? We must go back into Israel's history to see that this lack of understanding was present then also, yet God was trying to make clear His "Father" identity to them.

Examples of Sonship in the Old Testament

God as Father over Israel is a theme in the Old Testament. In the New Testament, He is Father of those He redeems through faith. This consistent theme serves as proof that the intimate relationship in Eden was not forever lost, as God was always Father to His children. He brought Israel out of slavery and later promised them a Messiah. God was already working for the restoration of men to that intimate relationship begun in Eden.

The following passages demonstrate God as Father to Israel.

"And you saw in the wilderness how the LORD your God carried you as a man carries his son all along the way you traveled until you reached this place." (Deuteronomy 1:31 HCS)[299]

"Keep in mind that the LORD your God has been disciplining you just as a man disciplines his son." (Deuteronomy 8:5 HCS)[300]

"You are sons of the LORD your God … you are a holy people belonging to the LORD your God. The LORD has chosen you to be His own possession out of all the peoples on the face of the earth." (Deuteronomy 14:2 HCS)[301]

"Is this how you repay the LORD, you foolish and senseless people? Isn't He your Father and Creator? Didn't He make you and sustain you?" (Deuteronomy 32:6 HCS)[302]

"Bring My sons from far away, and My daughters from the ends of the earth-everyone called by My name and created for My glory." (Isaiah 43:6-7 HCS)[303]

This is what the LORD, the Holy One of Israel and its Maker, says: "Ask Me what is to happen to My sons, and instruct Me about the work of My hands." (Isaiah 45:11 HCS)[304]

"They will come weeping, but I will bring them back with consolation ... for I am Israel's Father, and Ephraim is My firstborn." (Jeremiah 31:9 HCS)[305]

God as Father to His people, His sons and daughters, was already established in the Old Testament Scripture. But prior to the coming of the Messiah, there was enslavement to the law. As Paul said in Galatians 4:4, in the fullness of time for completing redemption, "He sent His Son, born of a woman, born under the Law, to redeem those under the Law, so that we might receive the adoption as sons." (HCS)[306] Jesus came to make us true sons and daughters, so that as new creations, we could be His agents on earth. We became messengers because He restored the relationship with man. Eden represents abundance and was meant as an environment to exercise freedom, not to endure restrictions. And that's our inheritance: freedom!

The great news of the gospel is that as God intended with Israel, He will be Father to His people. He calls them sons and daughters. They are not slaves. As Adam and Eve did in Eden, God's people serve Him as stewards, but they are full participants in the inheritance He promises as heirs of Abraham. What God began in Eden, He continued to do through Noah, Abraham, and Moses, to create for Himself a people to accomplish His purposes. In creating us—beings who were made for Eden and will experience Eden again—He prepares us to serve Him by giving us freedom and sonship. We must understand stewards are not servants. Jesus' obedience to the Father was done willingly. He did everything the Father sent Him for, believing that by Himself the Son could do nothing. He could only do what He saw the Father doing. By becoming sons and daughters, we become completely free to ask our Father to fulfill all He means for us to attempt. Once we are freed, then we become ambassadors of His victory over sin and death. Joining in this victory shows that we know Eden is ours and we must take back the freedom Jesus gives us by His victory over sin and death. He is calling you, as a new creation, to be His ambassadors, examples of a life reconciled to God.

9

Eden's Victory:
Ambassadors of a New Life.

Whether they have lived during wartime or not, most people have some understanding of what it means to win, to be victorious, over an enemy or opponent. But some of the most vivid pictures of victory are from war. In America, we have designated Memorial Day and Veterans Day holidays to celebrate those who fought, and who died, to secure our victories. Similarly, we celebrate our independence on July 4th. Meaningful moments in history make a lasting impression upon those who experienced celebrations of those moments. For this reason, moments which signified a big victory are named in ways that mark these occasions. These names, like V-E Day and V-J Day at the end of World War II, show their importance to our nation's freedom gained through victory. Naturally, there is great celebration when a nation's enemies are defeated. People take to the streets to rejoice, they hug their loves ones and even strangers. Those dates in our history also were an occasion to soberly remember the sacrifices made to achieve victory and to mourn over what was lost in the effort. All these reactions are appropriate when the efforts for freedom are of such a great magnitude.

The victory Jesus achieved over death, sin, and the devil, cost Him much. The price was His life. But in proclaiming on the cross "It is Finished," Jesus said the victory resulting from His death was secured forever. His work to secure our freedom from sin and death was complete. The celebration of victory in a war may be a mixture of emotions when losses are heavy. Some feel relief it has ended, and others feel satisfaction that their cause won. But we should have only joy and gratitude in Jesus' defeat of our enemy, for by it, He won our redemption back to God and His purpose for us. As a result of His victory, Jesus affirms His authority over the enemy, Satan.[307] Now that the victory over evil, death, and sin has been won, we are to enforce that victory. We enforce it by reminding ourselves, and our enemy, of Jesus' victory. We do this by serving the Conqueror as ambassadors. As new creations, our role as messengers of the victory of Christ is essential to our new life.

The Call to Be Ambassadors for Jesus

Before we can understand being ambassadors for Jesus because of His victory, the term ambassador needs defining. Ambassadors are emissaries of a sovereign nation, sent to enforce the policies of that nation as they engage in "diplomacy."

> ➢ They are afforded privileges in that country because of the nation they represent. One of those is diplomatic immunity.
> ➢ They establish a presence for their people among a foreign country and are advocates for those of their nation in that country. They are there to promote prosperity, peace, and protection for them.
> ➢ They are appointed by one in authority, and they serve at the pleasure of the one who appointed them.

There was a time—when I was interested in the political process, majoring in Public Policy and Political Science in college—that I thought about entering foreign service. The goal would be a diplomatic role with the hope of being appointed an ambassador. My grandparents, while serving in the US military in Europe, knew and spent time with ambassadors and other dignitaries. The lives I heard described sounded grand, important, influential. These traits were ones I wanted for my life and career. But working for our government, other than an internship in the US Congress, is not the path I followed. Yet, if I had better grasped the declaration Paul makes in 2 Corinthians 5 about how God sees our role in His purposes, I would have known I was already an ambassador of the King of Kings and Lord of Lords. While serving as a representative of my nation would have held honor, serving the wishes of the Creator of all things carries much more weight—and certainly carries eternal significance. Adam and Eve were His representatives in Eden. We were made for the same purpose: to represent Him on the earth. God is appealing to the world through us. We represent His interests, that all may witness His truth and be saved! We are ambassadors of the greatest government that ever existed. Isaiah 9:7 says His ruling authority will be vast, unending. He will establish His kingdom and sustain it forever. We have received an everlasting appointment to serve the interests of our Creator and Sustainer. So whatever our role is in the workplace, we are all ambassadors with supreme importance to the cause of the kingdom.

Ambassadors of Heaven

The parallels between being ambassadors of a nation, and of God Himself, are similar. As God called Adam and Eve to be illustrations of His provision and managers/stewards of creation, so He calls new creatures in Christ to be His messengers and stewards of grace.[308] We receive the privileges Jesus won for us, one of which is that our enemy must flee from us when we resist him.[309] Another is that we are given authority to trample on snakes and over all the power of the enemy and not be harmed.[310] Just like ambassadors are advocates in the nation where they serve, we are advocates of the reconciliation with God—we promote peace with God. Finally, in the same way ambassadors serve at the pleasure of the one who appointed them, so we serve at the Father's direction and pleasure.

Paul describes how God views us as vital carriers of His message by using the term ambassador.

> "For Christ's love compels us, since we have reached this conclusion: If One died for all, then all died. And He died for all so that those who live should no longer live for themselves, but for the One who died for them and was raised ... Therefore, if anyone is in Christ, he is a new creation; old things have passed away, and look, new things have come. Everything is from God, who reconciled us to Himself through Christ and gave us the ministry of reconciliation: That is, in Christ, God was reconciling the world to Himself, not counting their trespasses against them, and He has committed the message of reconciliation to us. Therefore, we are ambassadors for Christ, certain that God is appealing through us. We plead on Christ's behalf, 'Be reconciled to God.' He made the One who did not know sin to be sin for us, so that we might become the righteousness of God in Him." (2 Corinthians 5:14-15, 17-21 HCS)[311]

In becoming new creations, we become part of a chosen family advocating for a cause greater than our own life. Paul says in 2 Corinthians 5:15 that they should no longer live for themselves, but for the One who died for them.[312] We serve at the pleasure of the King of Kings, Jesus. We are His people; He bought us back from sin and death. Peter says in 1 Peter 2:9 that we are "are a chosen race, a royal priesthood, a holy nation, a people for His possession, so that you may proclaim the praises of the One who called you out of darkness into His marvelous light." (1 Peter 2:9 HCS)[313] We are His people, and we are to be proclaimers of what He accomplished to free us from sin's penalty. We are ministers of reconciliation.

The Ministry of Reconciliation: Ambassadors' Main Job

Jesus won the victory, and He gives us a role in His administration. We are ambassadors who enforce the victory. If the only point of rescuing us was to be in His presence, Jesus could just take us straight to heaven after we were reconciled to Him. But the goal of rescue is that with His presence inside us, we help others reconcile with God and become His children and heirs. How do we do that? We remain on earth to be His hands and feet, to be pictures of grace received. We get to help reconcile people to God. Paul says that as new creations, because the consequence of sin has been removed, and we are reconciled to God, God has made us ambassadors of His love, which offers reconciliation to all. God, in Christ, was reconciling the world to himself, and we are intermediaries of that reconciling activity.

Paul says we urge on Christ's behalf that people be reconciled to God. Paul is showing what a mighty commission we have from God. We represent God, who is both the party sinned against and the one offering reconciliation. Paul endured everything for the cause of Christ because he knew what power and promise the gospel carried.

Perseverance depends on knowing the God who called us, the identity He gives as the redeemed who've been forgiven, and the high privilege of carrying the message of reconciliation. But even those who know the blessings of being redeemed and count themselves ambassadors of God's reconciliation, faces obstacles to persevering.

Paul knew that because Jesus died to remove the barrier of sin that kept us apart from God, the love *behind that death* is what motivates us to obey God. If we really recognize Jesus' sacrificial love, it will produce an attitude of "here I am, send me" toward being an ambassador for Him. Once the call is understood, Paul expects us to be so compelled by knowing the magnitude of Jesus' love that it thrusts us into work as an ambassador.

Be a Good Soldier of Jesus

To show how dedicated we should be to representing God as His ambassadors on earth, Paul uses the analogy of a soldier. As a soldier accepts a commission into military service, so we accept our role in our service to our Master and His purpose. Just as ambassadors are under the authority of the nation who appoints them, so soldiers of God serve at His discretion and His command, engaged in His cause. Both military soldiers and those serving God engage in their service, believing the cause is greater than themselves. Soldiers follow the orders of their commander with victory as the goal. In our case, because Jesus already defeated our enemy, our assignment as soldiers of His cause is a reminder of a victory already won. We are like peacekeeping forces who remain in a nation after a war is won. Paul shows that serving our Lord requires absolute focus. He says soldiers of God don't engage in "civilian affairs" because they distract from the higher call. Paul says, "Suffer hardship with *me,* as a good soldier of Christ Jesus. No soldier in active service entangles himself in the affairs of everyday life, so that he may please the one who enlisted him."[314] There is a dedication to the One who called you into His service. Once again, our life is not our own. Like good military leaders focus on the objectives of winning the war, we are called to focus on the priorities of our Lord: the message of reconciliation to God.

I enjoy learning about history, including military history. There are many portraits of good soldiers. George Washington is an excellent example, especially during the Revolutionary War. Beginning with the campaigns in Boston and New York, Washington had a knack for outwitting the British when he was severely outnumbered in artillery, naval ships, and men. In a recent book on the conspiracy by his own honor guard to take his life, the author says of his escape from Brooklyn Heights in 1776 that Washington's army was "beaten, outfought, and stuck." Yet somehow "Washington led his troops to escape and survive."[315] "What made him great [in this war] was his sheer staying power, his total devotion to his army, his relentless sense of duty, and a stubborn refusal to ever give up."[316] The author says that several times in 1776 alone, the British could have forced his army into final defeat or capture. But that victory eluded the British. "They slowly learned a painful truth: as long as Washington and his army were out there somewhere, the British could never really win the war."[317]

Washington led the Americans to victory by his persistence in believing victory was worth the sacrifice, and by his dedication to the cause of liberty. Washington's actions in battle were vital in securing liberty for a new nation. They are an illustration of the truth that winning freedom requires great determination and sacrifice to achieve. It also requires action, even when facing improbable odds.

Fear of the odds did not keep Washington and his soldiers from engaging in their role for the cause they served. On July 2, 1776, with over 200 British ships in New York harbor, yet no naval ships for the Continentals, Washington issued this call to arms.

"The fate of unborn millions will now depend, under God, on the courage and conduct of this army. Our cruel and unrelenting enemy leaves us no choice, but a brave resistance or the most abject submission ... We have, therefore, to resolve to conquer or die."[318]

Certainly, Washington's words are not hyperbole. The new nation that was birthed in 1776 by the victory over the British did affect the lives of future millions. His resolve to carry out a war of rebellion against the enemy was born from a conviction that only by forming a new nation could the freedoms he desired be assured. Washington and his soldiers considered what they were fighting for worthy of death, so they fought, whatever their fate.

For the messengers of His kingdom, God's "army," the odds of a favorable outcome were much more dire than the Americans in 1776, outnumbered 200 to none. In Ephesians, Paul says all were dead in their sin apart from Jesus. The odds of our redemption to the life God meant for us were therefore hopeless. The Greek term Paul uses literally means lifeless, like a corpse. We were incapable of achieving life. But God, rich in mercy, made us alive with Him.[319] The price of our redemption was high.[320] The victory Jesus won over death and our enemy required the sacrifice of dying a criminal's painful death. Jesus was resolutely committed to His Father's plan for victory over the sin that separated us from His intention. Luke says he "set his face" toward Jerusalem, knowing the time of His sacrifice was near. His purpose was firm. Hebrews says we run our race of life "fixing our eyes on Jesus, the author and perfecter of faith, who for the joy set before

Him endured the cross ..." (Hebrews 12:2 NAS 1995)[321] Jesus knew what He was facing and endured it anyway, to achieve the victory it brought. With Jesus as our model, our resolve to remind our enemy of his defeat should be relentless. The enemy wants to steal, kill, and destroy lives, and is constantly looking for someone to devour. But he is defeated. As we submit to God, we must tenaciously resist the devil, firm in our faith that Jesus disarmed him, and therefore he must flee when we resist.

Tenacity and courage are traits of the good soldier of Jesus. But with the victory won, the outcome of serving Him with courage is sure! A victory implies there has been a struggle or war. The Bible uses a word to describe Jesus' victory on our behalf that means "victory through conquest." The victory earned, and the spoils gained from it, are because a war was won. Make no mistake, Jesus' incarnation and death were a declaration of war against the deceiver. By it, He declared that His death was enough to undo the curse brought onto mankind by sin in Eden. The difference between an earthly victory in wars between men, and what Jesus accomplished for us in disarming evil powers, is that once the sacrifice for sin was made, the outcome was secured!

Evidence of Jesus' Victory

So we would be sure the defeat of Satan was final, Paul gives a word picture of the totality of Jesus' victory over Satan and death.[322] In Colossians 2:14–15, Paul says Jesus nailed to the cross the decrees that were adverse to us because they showed we owed a debt we could not pay.[323] The decrees condemned us; they were a verdict against us. But when He disarmed the rulers and evil spiritual authorities, He changed the verdict over our life!

Not only did He win us back from the penalty of death, He made a declaration of victory by displaying them publicly as disgraced, defeated. Paul says Jesus "made a show of them."[324] Paul's words refer to the Roman example of the conquering general or emperor, dressed as the god Jupiter, leading a procession with his army. The humiliated captives, who have been stripped of their possessions which now belong to the Romans as spoils, are paraded before the victorious Romans.[325] This display, meant to disgrace those conquered, left no doubt who won the victory. This is what Jesus did to the enemy, Satan. He didn't just defeat him. He disarmed him and publicly displayed him as a defeated foe. Satan and his demons lost the battle for authority over men. In his letter to Corinth, Paul shows the necessity of Jesus' resurrection for our faith to have a firm foundation. Paul knew the death of the sinless One was the reason for the victory. Jesus paid the price for sin, and therefore, everything including Satan, sin, and death is put under Jesus' feet. Death was the last enemy, and it was conquered and abolished by the resurrection.[326]

Paul says that the Father triumphed over these evil powers and authorities by Jesus' sacrifice. Then, on top of all that, the Father gives us the victory Jesus earned over Satan and death! "But thanks be to God, who gives us the victory through our Lord Jesus Christ."[327] Jesus won the victory, and because He is in us, we get the benefit of that victory! Satan cannot hold us in sin and death anymore. John says that "The Son of God appeared for this purpose, to destroy the works of the devil."[328] That is what we proclaim as ambassadors and soldiers. Jesus won, and because He is in us, we share in the victory.

Preview of the Victory Was in Eden

One incredible aspect of this victory is that God promised a Son of Man would be victorious over Satan. This was spoken at the time the sin in the garden was committed! Satan's judgment was proclaimed all the way back in Genesis 3:15, at the time of the fall of men. It says that an heir of Adam would crush Satan's head. The verdict of the Father is that Satan will bruise His heel, but Jesus, the Redeemer, will crush Satan's head.[329] Jesus would be the heir of Adam who would crush Satan's head. Jesus would be "bruised," crushed for our sin, but His death and resurrection paid the penalty for sin and put us on His "winning side."

Jesus said on the cross, "It Is Finished." Not "it is mostly done, but I need you to do the rest." No, he took away the sting of death and of sin, and he gave us the resulting victory. He is the Victor. John gives us a picture in Revelation of the conquering Jesus as Victor.

"His head and His hair were white like white wool, like snow; and His eyes were like a flame of fire. His feet *were* like burnished bronze, when it has been made to glow in a furnace, and His voice *was* like the sound of many waters. In His right hand He held seven stars, and out of His mouth came a sharp two-edged sword; and His face was like the sun shining in its strength. When I saw Him, I fell at His feet like a dead man. And He placed His right hand on me, saying, 'Do not be afraid; I am the first and the last, and the living One; and I was dead, and behold, I am alive forevermore, and I have the keys of death and of Hades.'"[330]

"The victor: I will give him the right to sit with Me on My throne, just as I also won the victory and sat down with My Father on His throne." (Revelation 3:21 HCS)[331]

"Then one of the elders said to me, 'Stop crying. Look! The Lion from the tribe of Judah, the Root of David, has been victorious so that He may open the scroll and its seven seals.'" (Revelation 5:5 HCS)[332]

He is the Victor. It is time to take back the freedom He won for us. The war was won, and we were given all the spoils of that victory. We received a new commission from that victory also: to be His ambassadors to the world. We simply have to enforce what He gained for us. We do this simply by speaking the truth. We state that we are reconciled to God. We tell the enemy to flee because we resist him. And in gratitude for receiving the benefit of His victory, we serve as God's ambassadors, and as soldiers, we fight the good fight of faith.

Ambassadors Need Not Fear

Because Jesus has won, we have no reason to fear. There is literally a Scripture verse for every day of the year telling us not to fear. A key to ambassadors not fearing is to know that everything we ever need, we already have. "His divine power has given us everything we need for life and godliness through the knowledge of Him who calls us, by his own glory and goodness." (2 Peter 1:3 HCS)[333] There is no way to fail because the victory has already been secured. Unfortunately, the way we live often shows we don't understand we have already been given everything we need for life in Him and are guaranteed the benefit of His victory. There isn't something "out there" that still eludes us—a magic key that unlocks our path to serving Him with lasting impact. It's when we focus on being more than conquerors through Him who loves us that we realize we truly are victorious.[334]

Motivation to Be Ambassadors

What we have, as children of God and heirs of His promises, is far greater than what armies engaging in battle have. *The outcome of the war for mankind's redemption is secure, and the fate of those who embrace the victory is assured!* The battle has already been won. We have misunderstood what "fighting the good fight of faith" means. It's not about securing victory over our flesh or the enemy. The enemy has been defeated, and we are no longer under obligation to the flesh. When we see the kingdom message as a treasure waiting to be found, we will be motivated to fight the good fight. Jesus told a parable of the kingdom that compares the discovery of God's life and its purposes to a treasure. The man recognizes such worth in the treasure that, upon finding it, he buys the field containing it, at the cost of all he has.[335] It is why Paul can urge the Ephesians to live a life worthy of the calling they have received.[336] We have all the peace, love, and joy to gain by fulfilling our calling to live as ambassadors. To fulfill what He called us to do is to experience the abundant, eternal life He came to give. We don't just receive God's mercy, we are also, as we said, His ambassadors, carriers of that mercy and of the transformation that results from receiving that mercy. God is making things right in His creation by reconciling men to Himself. And through an indwelling Spirit who carries the power of Jesus' resurrected life, men are made right with Him, so they can grow in their role as ambassadors of the grace and mercy they have received.

The Role of Hope for Ambassadors

One of the foundational truths in the message of the gospel is that hope is the anchor of the soul. We are ambassadors of that hope. Our lives are evidence that redemption exists, and that eternal union with God will be experienced by all who persevere unto salvation. The despair we see in America—the suicides, addictions, and depression among prominent people, and among many others not in the public eye—could be attributed to a loss of hope. To lose one's own faith in order to experience greater things in life means hope is no longer an anchor. In other words, their current despair is not surpassed by the hope of something greater in the future.

In contrast, what is the hope that followers of Jesus are to hold onto? For Paul, the hope is the return of Jesus to judge evil and to fulfill the promise to believers. It is not heaven only, but His return to earth.[337] His second coming is not for the purpose of offering Himself for sin again, but to usher in eternity for the believer.

> "And there will be signs in sun and moon and stars, and on the earth distress of nations in perplexity because of the roaring of the sea and the waves, people fainting with fear and with foreboding of what is coming on the world. For the powers of the heavens will be shaken. And then they will see the Son of Man coming in a cloud with power and great glory. Now when these things begin to take place, straighten up and raise your heads, because your redemption is drawing near." (Luke 21:25-28 ESV)[338]

One task of the children of God is to be ambassadors of the fact that God is through Jesus reconciling the world to Himself. And that our hope is not primarily in a place, but in a person, who loved us and gave Himself for us. He will return to finish what he started: the redemption of a people for God's own possession, saints, ones called into a mission with the Creator of the universe. We are part of a new and living way, and we are responsible, and urged, to strengthen our hold on that future, and to help others to do so. To serve as an ambassador of the greatest message ever proclaimed, we must be empowered by joy. This joy gives us strength to step into our role, and it comes from knowing God loves us and gave us real purpose.[339] Jesus Himself showed us why this message is the greatest ever known, and why it should produce joy. To explain, we can turn to the scene of Jesus on the cross, flanked by the two thieves.

Jesus the First Enforcer of the Victory: The Example of the Cross

The last moments of Jesus on the cross are remarkable for what He says as He was suffering. Though films have portrayed the gravity of that moment, I need reminding just how revolutionary the final moments of Jesus' earthly life were. When Jesus was crucified, He was hung between two thieves. One thief on the cross responded to the other's mockery of Jesus being a Messiah who couldn't save Himself. This thief recognized he was getting what he deserved.[340] But he asked Jesus to "remember me when you come into your kingdom."[341] The thief's words were a statement filled with hope; they were not a question of "will you bring me to your kingdom?" He knew that if Jesus was indeed King over a kingdom, He had the right to allow someone into it. Jesus responded to the thief with "Truly I say to you, today you will be with me in Paradise."[342]

Luke 23 is written about a thief who was also to be killed that day. We are left to wonder why the thief concluded, though others had failed to see, that Jesus' true identity, purpose, and authority were as the Son of God. Perhaps it was Jesus asking His Father to forgive those who were nailing Him to the cross. Maybe it was Jesus' silence in the face of those laughing at and mocking Him. Or possibly it was the ridicule of the other condemned man, who asked Jesus to save himself, and them, if He really was Messiah.[343]

For any or all of these reasons, the thief sensed that Jesus was telling the truth about Himself, that He was Messiah. He asked Jesus to show him grace and deliver him into His kingdom. Cynics may say the thief's words were a last ditch effort to justify his worthiness to avoid death, hedging his bets that there was life after death for him. But I think that the thief genuinely saw Jesus as the Son of God, and we know Jesus could see into the hearts of men in order to gauge this. I believe His assurance to the thief is based on seeing his genuine belief. The thief called him Lord, asking, "When you come into your kingdom, will you take me into it?" In effect, will you receive me, an undeserving man who has done much wrong in my life, into your eternity?

Jesus' promise to the thief that he will be with Him in paradise is evidence that new life in Christ is available to all. A man is sentenced to death by earthly authorities for his crimes, yet Jesus says he will be in paradise that day. Man was meant for that paradise, in Jesus' presence. In what we read, this man had not prayed certain words of confession of sin or been baptized. He had not been taught about what the new man looked like and certainly had no time to develop the traits Paul says resemble new life. But Jesus judged that he was ready to cast off the old man and wanted the life Jesus could provide. That was enough.

The extravagant love of God is the hope for each of us, like the thief, to be restored to Eden. And the death of Jesus is proof of that love for it allows for the reconciliation between God and man. Reconciliation is the ultimate standard by which a life is measured. As Paul said, God makes his plea through us to be reconciled to God.[344] The means of getting to the presence of God is by claiming the reconciliation Jesus' sacrifice provides, recognizing Jesus for who He is, and acknowledging His Kingship. Jesus is a sinless King who did not deserve to die but gave Himself up for us.

In one sense, this story is a reflection of the contrast between the message of Jesus and that of religion. There were plenty of views that opposed Jesus in his day, from Pharisees to Sadducees to many in between, who felt if they just got the conclusions about life and the expression of faith right, they could please God and show off their devoutness to each other. The history of man is full of thieves and murderers. Adam and Eve were in essence thieves; they took fruit from a tree that God had forbidden. Cain was a murderer. We don't have to get even ten chapters into the Bible to find these examples. But the point of Jesus telling the thief, "today you will be with Me in Paradise," is that the life of Eden, the life we sinners were meant for, is not obtained by obeying a formula. No system of theology is going to get us into His paradise, the place He went to prepare for us. The re-entry to perfection like in Eden is gained by seeing Jesus as the Messiah, the One who suffered for us on a horrible cross, to bring us close again to Father's best. There is no stopping the effect of His generous love. I am sure there were many watching Jesus' proclamation with indignation and even horror. They may have screamed to Jesus as He suffered, "that man doesn't deserve your love." Jesus could have responded with "Well, neither do you." But "deserving it" is not the qualifier for receiving His love. The purpose we were made for in Eden is the reason for Jesus' sacrificial act of death on a cross to secure our eternal relationship with the Father. It is why He humbled himself and lived as a human. The effect of the sin in the garden was severe. The redemption plan had to involve the offering of the only sinless One who would ever live.

So the thief hoped in Jesus, and Jesus set that hope as a seal over his life.[345] This one belongs to Me! I, Jesus, am the door to the sheepfold. No one comes to the Father but by Me. So if I say this man will be with Me where I am, he will!

How does that scene connect to Eden? Because the moment someone tells you that eternity with God is based on what religion you practice, what church denomination you affiliate with, what version of the Bible you use, or what you have done to please God, you must remind them of this story in Scripture. Jesus didn't ask the thief to explain any of these matters to Him before He changed his future forever. Without faith, it is impossible to please Him, for the one who comes to God must do what? He must believe that God is, and that He rewards those who seek Him. That's what the thief did. He believed Jesus had done nothing deserving of death. He had faith that Jesus was in a position (held the authority) to determine his eternity. And he believed God was a rewarder, giving life after death through a King who was willingly dying in order to fill up His kingdom with undeserving, but fully-loved, future sons and daughters.

This moment in Jesus' life has everything to do with the message of this book because it demonstrates than even the vilest sins cannot prevent a person from experiencing God's best if they will but see Jesus for who He is and accept the redemption that His death and resurrection provide. In place of a need to be *deserving* of Eden, Jesus is looking for those full of faith, ready to "drop their nets" and follow Him back to the Father. For "the one who has seen Me has seen the

Father."[346] And "if the Son sets you free, you really will be free."[347] Jesus is the victor, and He has set us free from death!

So let's grab hold of the truth that restores joy, which radiates from the fact that Jesus wasn't asking the thief to "clean up his act" in those final moments, nor was He even making the question of righteousness and eternity about the man himself. Jesus could see by his request that the man knew such a request would and could only be answered with "yes" by a God who would send His own Son to die for undeserving sinners. Which of us followers of this same Jesus wouldn't want to be His ambassador?

10

Skeptics of Eden:
The Question of Suffering
and Evil

E arlier chapters in this book have included many promises for our life in Christ. These promises are evidence of how good the news is that God's plan is to redeem us to our Eden purpose. So "what is the catch?" Is it "too good to be true" that we can regain the purpose God ordained in Eden? What do we have to do, or give up, in order to get it? The Bible does speak about evil and its effect on the world and the life God intends for us. It does include the idea of the restoration of all things, and of our renewal to His purpose for us as ambassadors and stewards on earth. But what about the hard realities we see in the world today? What about war, genocide, famine, racial and ethnic violence, and terrorist activity waged between groups of people? How about natural disasters that Scripture says will be on the rise in the last days? How about a global health concern like the one experienced in 2020? Does the belief that mankind was made for Eden fail to account for these realities?

There are biblical passages describing the difficulty of living a Christ-centered life in the midst of evil.[348] Paul's ministry involved suffering for proclaiming that our life can be empowered by Jesus based on His substitutionary death. As I've noted, the life "in Christ" that Paul describes was a radical change from his previous expressions of his devoutly held belief in God. But his writings give us clues on how he viewed his new life in Jesus and its operation within the world around him. Even though Paul's world was corrupted by sin, as is our world today, the future for the believer is not altered by evil.

View of Circumstances Is Shaped by View of the Master

Paul knew his message was divinely revealed, and therefore was entirely true and trustworthy.[349] This enabled—even emboldened—Paul to proclaim truth without regard for his personal safety or reputation because the God who appeared to him supernaturally became the Master of his life. We see Paul's commitment to serving this Master in 2 Corinthians 11:23-28, where he defends, from his own hardships, what serving Jesus may result in.

> "Are they servants of Christ?—I speak as if insane—I more so; in far more labors, in far more imprisonments, beaten times without number, often in danger of death. Five times I received from the Jews thirty-nine lashes. Three times I was beaten with rods, once I was stoned, three times I was shipwrecked, a night and a day I have spent in the deep...I have been in labor and hardship, through many sleepless nights, in hunger and thirst, often without food, in cold and exposure. Apart from such external things, there is the daily pressure on me of concern for all the churches." (NAS 1995)[350]

As he leaves Ephesus, as recorded in Acts, Paul says,

"And now, behold, bound by the Spirit, I am on my way to Jerusalem, not knowing what will happen to me there, except that the Holy Spirit solemnly testifies to me in every city, saying that bonds and afflictions await me. But I do not consider my life of any account as dear to myself, so that I may finish my course and the ministry which I received from the Lord Jesus, to testify solemnly of the gospel of the grace of God … For I did not shrink from declaring to you the whole purpose of God."[351]

Paul's commitment to His Lord was tested and found true. He did not abandon his call when the circumstances became very challenging.

Paul's View of Evil in the World

Paul believed that the presence of evil in the world meant we would suffer as we serve Jesus on this earth. He demonstrated, by recounting his personal history of suffering for gospel, that such hardship is worth the cost. Because of the magnitude of the gift he found in Jesus, a new and living way of relating to God, Paul encouraged us to share in Jesus' suffering as we serve God.[352] The world, even believers, may have misunderstood him or rebuffed his message, but Paul was not deterred, for He knew that God proclaimed him a servant to the gentiles to carry the news of God's plan to restore mankind to His original purpose among creation. He prayed in Colossians 4 that God would open a door for the message.[353] For Paul, personal hardship is worth it for more people to know the offer of redemption.

Paul taught that the evil of men would increase as the return of Christ drew nearer. In relating to an increasingly evil world, he wanted followers of Jesus to persevere in their pursuit of His ways, no matter the condition of the culture around them.

In 2 Timothy, Paul expresses his view on what our response should be to the increase of evil as the return of Jesus approaches. That response is to endure all situations as you serve God.[354] He says to expect suffering.

Rather than focusing on hardship, Paul challenges believers in the last days to cling to the fact that God's truth is actively maturing them to face whatever comes. Not all people will persevere in their faith but will deny God's power. Yet His power is required for faith that endures. Our task is to continue in the truth we are convinced of and to allow the Bible to teach and train us to flourish. It can equip us for everything He has for us to do, in spite of those who fall into evil.

> "But realize this, that in the last days difficult times will come. For men will be lovers of self … lovers of pleasure rather than lovers of God, holding to a form of godliness, although they have denied its power; Avoid such men as these … Indeed, all who desire to live godly in Christ Jesus will be persecuted. But evil men and impostors will proceed *from bad* to worse, deceiving and being deceived. You, however, continue in the things you have learned and become convinced of, knowing from whom you have learned *them,* and that from childhood you have known the sacred writings which are able to give you the wisdom that leads to salvation through faith which is in Christ Jesus. All Scripture is inspired by God and profitable for teaching, for reproof, for correction, for training in righteousness; so that the man of God may be adequate, equipped for every good work."[355]

There are several points here that demonstrate that the circumstances around us in the latter days do not prevent the fulfillment of God's purposes for the believer.

> A believer may suffer hardship—even imprisonment as a criminal—but the word of God is not imprisoned.
> In the last days difficult times will come. For men will be lovers of self.
> All who desire to live godly in Christ Jesus will be persecuted.
> We must continue in the things we have learned and become convinced of.
> God's Word is enough to make us adequately equipped to face whatever comes.

The love of things other than God will be on the rise, and we should expect some persecution. But rather than being drawn into the deception of loving self so intently that, in order to protect ourselves, we shrink back from serving God, we should continue in what we know is true about God's purpose for us. Our life is not without struggle or suffering. But persevering in our efforts to fulfill our call as ambassadors honors Him who enlists us. By refusing to get entangled in situations that don't serve His purposes, we serve our Lord well.

For Paul, focused obedience in his role as an ambassador resulted in imprisonment. "For this I am an ambassador in chains. Pray that I might be bold enough in Him to speak as I should."[356] "This" refers to making known the gospel. Though he was in chains, God's Word is not chained. It equips us for the good work we are called to. Paul was assuring the believers in Ephesus that hardship will come, but it does not negate our call to be ambassadors.

We Are Lights in Darkness

In 2 Timothy 3:17, Paul says the Bible is profitable for training us in righteousness. It is a tool for maturing us in our new identity as those crucified with Christ. When it comes to God's purposes, Paul tells the church at Philippi that they must "work out" their salvation, knowing God is at work in them. The goal of that sanctifying process would be to stand out as lights amidst the crooked generation around them.[357] In order for the faith of those at Philippi to grow and therefore be proven genuine, Paul was willing to be poured out on their behalf. He was convinced that God is faithful even when persecution comes. He knew that by seeking to please His Master, Jesus, he would not "run in vain." By following our Master like Paul did, we will confront situations where evil is at work. Because Jesus is empowering us, we can stand firm against evil and fulfill His purposes.

I recently saw the movie *Priceless*. The main character realizes he has stepped into, and unwittingly contributed to, a perverse world of human trafficking. The movie is ultimately about the choices we make to oppose evil even in its most heinous forms, and how committed to those choices we are. Will we choose to influence the situations we are aware of even if taking action seems to affect only one or a few lives? Or will we be so overwhelmed by the size and force of evil that we draw back from exerting our influence out of fear or apathy that our action can't affect "the system"?

We need examples of what living a "crucified with Christ" life looks like in a world full of need for God's light. Nicole Nordeman's song "Dear Me" reflects her journey in understanding what characterizes "faith in action" in light of human need. She writes to her younger self about how time has changed her perspective on relating to the poor, and the privileges we enjoy, like safety from war, living in freedom, and being educated. The lyrics in the song encourage cries for justice for victims, love for those who experience loss, and esteem for those who defend our country's freedom. We should love everyone we encounter because we have been loved and *He* is love. His love goes into places we have not imagined, and He wants us to carry His love there too. Nordeman says, "And you cannot imagine all the places you'll see Jesus. But you'll find Him everywhere you thought He wasn't supposed to go, So, go, go!"[358] Whenever we go where He leads us, Jesus affirms that acts of love that encourage people to live out their God-given purpose are not wasted because they are done unto Him.[359]

What Desire for Redemption Says about Good and Evil

Jesus commands us to be lights in the darkness.[360] But trying to shine in the midst of evil is not easy, nor is it welcomed by those in darkness for they resist light.[361] Creation itself is under the weight of darkness. Just as we stand firm against evil while working toward the purpose of God while we wait for the final state of our restoration to Eden, so creation is waiting. Paul says in Romans 8 "that the creation itself also will be set free from its slavery to corruption. For we know that the whole creation groans and suffers the pains of childbirth together until now. And not only this, but also we ourselves, having the first fruits of the Spirit, even we ourselves groan within ourselves, waiting eagerly for *our* adoption as sons, the redemption of our body." (Romans 8:21-23 NAS 1995)[362]

We wait for the redemption of our body, for freedom from the fallen nature of this world. The creation also groans for its redemption from the effects of the evil activity of "the ruler of this world." We have been given the first fruits of our inheritance: the Holy Spirit within us. And we long for more fruit from that gift as He empowers us to fulfill our purpose. Think of tasting the first fruit of a new season of the year. What does having your first blueberry, peach, or melon do to you? Doesn't it create a desire for more of it? Our desire for redemption comes from what we were made for, and what we have already been given.

Because of the perfection we were made for, a desire for all things to be "right" was planted in our hearts by God. Why else would Hollywood borrow its imagery of loss and redemption from the biblical story? Some of the most enduring and successful films have redemption as their main theme.[363] How many of these movies have a person in distress who is rescued or restored to their rightful place by a heroic figure? For us, that hero is Jesus! He is removing us from slavery to corruption, as Paul says of creation in Romans 8:21, into the glorious freedom marked for His children.

And Nordeman's point in "Dear Me" is that rather than taking restoration for granted, we should work for it! We can be His hands and feet to those on earth who either don't know the promises of God and what they say about our identity and authority or who are not experiencing these promises. We should go into the world and love deeply because He is love, and His love reaches out to who welcome redemption.

Until the return of Jesus at the time known only to the Father, the need for overcoming evil with good remains. And we, His ambassadors, are the instruments He uses to bring light into the darkness. The increasing depth of the darkness only increases the need for us to fulfill our role. The power of Jesus working through our "new man," to model restored union with God, is essential to shining our light against the world's evil. By doing the good works you were uniquely gifted for by the God who made you for Eden, you participate in good overcoming evil.

To answer the skeptic, the good news is true, that living as new creations renews us to our God-given purpose. It requires that we let God's Word and God's Spirit direct us, our thoughts and our actions, as we no longer live but Christ lives His life in us.

Fruit that Results from God's Life Maturing in Us

Living within our purpose, as Christ lives His life in us, produces fruit that remains. But that does require action on our part. Paul exhorts his hearers concerning their new identity. For Paul, these actions result from receiving our new identity in Jesus. These actions are part of shining light against the darkness.

"Let's not become discouraged in doing good, for in due time we will reap if we do not grow weary. So then, while we have opportunity, let us do good to all people, and especially to those who are of the household of the faith."[364]

"That, in reference to your former manner of life, you lay aside the old self, which is being corrupted in accordance with the lusts of deceit, and that you be renewed in the spirit of your mind, and put on the new self, which in *the likeness of* God has been created in righteousness and holiness of the truth." (Ephesians 4:22-24 NAS 1995)[365]

"Do not lie to one another, since you laid aside the old self with its evil practices, and have put on the new self who is being renewed to a true knowledge according to the image of the One who created him—a renewal in which there is no distinction between Greek and Jew, circumcised and uncircumcised, barbarian, Scythian, slave and freeman, but Christ is all, and in all." (Colossians 3:9-11 NAS 1995)[366]

"Finally, be strong in the Lord and in the strength of His might. Put on the full armor of God, so that you will be able to stand firm against the schemes of the devil."[367]

Paul told us to do these things as new men and women belonging to God. This "Christ in me" life is real, and it can be the defining characteristic of your life. Jesus meant this offer of Galatians 2:20 for all who would embrace it. If we will live according to our inheritance, and let God work in us mightily, then we will experience now the life we were meant for.[368]

Paul says to the Corinthians that we are a fragrant aroma of our Lord to the world.

"But thanks be to God, who always leads us in triumph in Christ, and manifests through us the sweet aroma of the knowledge of Him in every place. For we are a fragrance of Christ to God among those who are being saved and among those who are perishing; to the one an aroma from death to death, to the other an aroma from life to life. And who is adequate for these things? … we speak in Christ in the sight of God."[369]

We aren't adequate in our old selves to be a pleasing fragrance, but "in Him," Paul says we are a fragrance of Christ to God among those who are being saved. Our lives become a "scent" of God to the perishing. It's not our sermons, not our gospel presentations, not our altar calls, but rather how much we carry the scent of having been with Jesus that measures how much Jesus manifests through us.

If Paul can say that he considers what He has given up in favor of knowing Jesus to be trash, and Isaiah says his righteousness is like filthy rags, then our lives must be a reflection of "Jesus living in us" for them to have a fragrance that draws others. For Paul, "whatever things were gain to me, those things I have counted as loss for the sake of Christ. More than that, I count all things to be loss in view of the surpassing value of knowing Christ Jesus my Lord, for whom I have suffered the loss of all things, and count them but rubbish so that I may gain Christ."[370]

There Is Hope for Redemption for All

The experience of suffering in our fallen world does not diminish the promises contained in being made for Eden. As Paul said, whatever we count as loss in our desire to follow Jesus, those things hold no value in comparison to Him living His life through us. Paul's own story is a reminder that even inflicting suffering on God's chosen ones does not prevent a person from enjoying the offer of redemption. Paul was a persecutor of The Way of Christ and was present at, as well as had consented to, the killing of Stephen.[371] He was holding the cloaks of those hurling the stones. He had, at that time, not believed in Jesus as the Messiah. In 1 Timothy 1:15-16, he calls himself the worst of sinners, saying

> "This saying is trustworthy deserving of full acceptance: "Christ Jesus came into the world to save sinners"- and I am the worst of them. But I received mercy for this reason, so that in me, the worst of them, Christ Jesus might demonstrate His extraordinary patience as an example to those who would believe in Him for eternal life." (HCS)[372]

Paul says God showed him mercy as the chief of sinners. Adopt Paul's way of seeing his former life as you consider your own. Before Jesus was revealed to him supernaturally,

Paul felt his former way of life was pleasing to God. After his encounter with Jesus he had a new understanding of the value of his new life to God. His value was not in his deeds, but in his identity as God's child. Paul taught that we must walk "worthy" of this new identity as those belonging to God. Indeed, Paul says "therefore I, the prisoner of the Lord, urge you to walk in a manner worthy of the calling with which you have been called ..."[373]

Paul thinks there is a responsibility that comes with the pursuit of Eden; we are to walk worthy of our call as stewards. To those who are not part of God's family, the cost of our pursuit of that call can seem foolish. Paul anticipates this reaction and the mindset behind it. He says in 1 Corinthians 1:26–30:

> "For consider your calling, brethren, that there were not many wise according to the flesh, not many mighty, not many noble; but God has chosen the foolish things of the world to shame the wise, and God has chosen the weak things of the world to shame the things which are strong, and the base things of the world and the despised God has chosen, the things that are not, so that He may nullify the things that are, so that no man may boast before God. But by His doing you are in Christ Jesus, who became to us wisdom from God, and righteousness and sanctification, and redemption." (NAS 1995)

As we think about what the gospel says about us and about God, and what Him living in and through us means, we need to come to terms with this passage in 1 Corinthians 1. There is a dynamic difference between how God views the worth of the things of this world and how He values the "things that are not." Because of that difference, Paul explains we can boast only in God. We live in a world that loves to boast in itself and assigns value to athletes and entertainers far more than it does to teachers and custodians. But the idea that God chooses the weak and foolish to shame the strong is meant to prepare us for the realities of God's kingdom that we find so hard to fathom. His values are wholly different than our world's. So are His promises, in the midst of a world awaiting redemption.

Suffering and Promise

As I said, I am not untouched by suffering. I have watched loved ones go through much pain and physical need. I have witnessed the enemy "steal, kill, and destroy" in people's lives through premature death. But I have also seen firsthand the intervention of God, intersecting their need and inspiring their faith to move mountains, and I've seen people rise up and refuse to be ruled by their circumstances. Fear keeps us under a situation. Faith encourages us to confess "that which is not as though it were," as Abraham did.

When my wife was told for the second time she had cancer, she set her heart to the truth of God's promises. She spoke Psalm 118:17 over herself from the moment she heard a diagnosis, which says "I will not die, but I will live and proclaim what the LORD has done." (HCS)[374] Live and not die.

She spoke the truth she wanted to occur. She didn't deny she had cancer. That would be calling that which "is" as though it were not. That is not what Romans says Abraham did. When faced with the fact that his body was old, as was Sarah's, he called himself "father of many nations" before he had a child. Paul says,

"... in God's presence he believed that God can raise the dead and call into being things that don't even exist yet. Against all odds, when it looked hopeless, Abraham believed the promise and **expected God to fulfill it. He took God at his word**, and as a result he became the father of many nations. God's declaration over him came to pass... In spite of being nearly one hundred years old when the promise of having a son was made, **his faith was so strong that it could not be undermined by the fact** that he and Sarah were incapable of conceiving a child. **He never stopped believing God's promise**, for he was made strong in his faith to father a child. And because he was mighty in faith and convinced that God had all the power needed to fulfill his promises, Abraham glorified God!" (emphasis mine) Romans 4:17–21 (TPT)[375]

The degree of suffering we experience by living in a world awaiting its final redemption does not negate the promises of God. No advanced age, as with Abraham, or advanced cancer, as with my wife, is beyond the promise. In speaking of man's faith versus God's faithfulness to His word, Paul says, "God must be true, even if everyone is a liar." (Romans 3:4 HCS)[376] Suffering neither denies what God says about His creation, nor limits what His word says is possible for His children. My wife's story is still being written as she did live to proclaim God's works and His goodness. Taking God at His word, as Abraham did, is vital to fulfilling His purpose as we await the full redemption of all creation.

Our View of Suffering Hinges on Our View of God

The level to which the evil in the world will influence our belief that we were Made for Eden depends on what we expect God to reveal through His intimate relationship with us. The promises of what will be ours once we experience the new heaven and new earth are staggering. But do we really believe God is preparing such a glorious future for His children as He says? Jesus says if it were not so, He would have told us.[377] What are we prepared to see? What does the nature of the new heaven and earth say about God's nature?

Author Frederick Buechner says, "People are prepared for a God who strikes hard bargains but not for a God who gives as much for an hour's work as for a day's."[378] He refers to the parable of the vineyard in Matthew 20. The generosity of God toward those who are hired to work the vineyard is a vivid picture of those who repent and look to Him for their direction and their strength, whenever that occurs in their life. That generosity allows the promise of a restored future to give us hope. And ultimately our hope is in His goodness, out of which He fulfills His promises.

What are many of us prepared for when it comes to God's actions toward His children? Do we see Him like the father in the parable of the prodigal, ready to kill the fatted calf because we have returned to Him, or do we see Him only as judge? Do we expect Him to give us a stone instead of bread when we pray? Or are we like Isaiah and Paul, that once we understand the enormity of what God is offering, we are ready to enlist to be His representatives, His sons, and His friends? I believe when we undergo the surrender of our old self, and actively engage in having Jesus live His life in us, we will see the greater works Jesus prophesied for those who follow Him. Life comes only from death, and the aroma of Jesus coming through us requires that I lose my life for His sake. This act of humility toward He who died for me unleashes the power of God in me.

Paul's message about gaining Jesus and the life we have in Him is one of simplicity. Paul is responsible for writing the most letters adopted into the Canon of Scripture; he could boast of his superior status in the eyes of men. Yet his focus is not on himself and his worthiness. His eye is firmly on what God did in him as a result of his experience on the Damascus road, and how God called him to serve the body of Christ.

It is from that experience, and the subsequent revelation by God's Spirit, that Paul believed what God had promised concerning His redemptive plan. Paul rejoices that God had taken him, a persecutor of The Way of Jesus, and made him an apostle of reconciliation. He says superior speech and persuasive words of wisdom were not his goal. It is the simple message of Jesus, giving His life to buy back men and women for God, that transforms lives.

Whose Will Do You Choose?

The decision facing each of us is whose will we choose to follow. The first Adam chose in the Garden of Eden "not your will but mine." The second Adam, Jesus, chose in Gethsemane "not my will but yours, Father." Romans 5:9–21 describes in detail the differences in the two Adam identities.[379] The choice to follow God's will in our lives really is the greatest proof that we believe in the life of "Christ in me" as described in Galatians 2:20. Will we listen to the voice of the enemy who tries to entice us to act contrary to the truth of the Bible? Or will we take captive the thoughts that arise from the enemy as he attempts to lead us into sin? When we follow God's voice only, and refuse the tactics or schemes of the enemy, we are following the way of Jesus. The truth of the cross is that "God made the only one who did not know sin to become sin for us, so that we might become the righteousness of God through our union with Him." (2 Corinthians 5:21 TPT)[380] We don't pin our hope on what *we* can produce from our lives, but on what God can bring forth from our lives through Jesus. We rely on the life and faith of the One who died for us, who lives today at the right hand of the Father. This is our only hope.

Therefore, the truth of the Eden life is not contradicted by the existence of suffering. The life Jesus and Paul describe is available to all no matter the amount of wrongdoing or suffering one has lived through or will experience. And He who started the work in us will be faithful to complete the redemptive work which enables our lives to reflect honor back to Him. He completes what He has begun in us so that our lives can be as at original creation: good and pleasing to God. Paul sums up the dynamic of Christ working in us to bring honor to God this way: "work out your own salvation with fear and trembling; for it is God who is at work in you, both to will and to work for *His* good pleasure.[381] Since no amount of evil or suffering on earth can nullify His redemptive plan, He will fulfill the promises of Revelation. God promises Eden will be restored and we will experience it!

11

Eden Restored: The Future for Overcomers

The focus of this book has been on God's original purpose for Adam and Eve on earth and how that God-appointed role still serves as our mandate, as we are His representatives on earth. The role we play in God reconciling the world to Himself is significant according to Paul in 2 Corinthians 5. Adam and Eve's function in God's Garden of Eden was meant to be lived in His intimate presence. As we steward God's creation and serve as His messengers on the earth, we too are to live by the power of His presence, not only with us but inside us, because Jesus reconciled us to God. His life and sacrificial death restore mankind to the same intimate relationship with God that Adam and Even enjoyed in the garden.

Past, Present, and Future Views of Eden

Let's refresh some key thoughts about our theme. First, God made us in His image, and placed the first man and woman He created in the environment He designed for them. Their sin, brought on by believing the enemy's words that were contrary to what God told them, produced a consequence: separation from that perfect environment. But the promised relationship with God and His purpose for us was not lost forever. God promised to Abraham a nation as an inheritance, and he believed God would fulfill it. Because Abraham trusted God's Word, God called him righteous. Through a future heir of Abraham, God began bringing mankind back to all He had intended when He made man. He gave Israel a promise of a land flowing with milk and honey that He would empower them to possess. Despite all the ways Israel disobeyed what God wanted them to do, He promised to deliver them and to bless them. He promised that an heir of David would come who would deliver them and, just as He promised to Abraham, all the nations would be blessed through Him. That heir, Jesus, did come, lived a sinless life, and died to pay the penalty of all the sin of mankind, including those in the garden. This same Jesus was victorious over Satan and removed us from underneath the curse of sin and death. He also made us part of His family, to rule alongside Him in His kingdom, and He gives us strength to do everything He prepared for us to do before we ever embraced His grace.

As a result of the cross, we are righteous and restored to the relationship with God we were always meant for. Because we die with Him and are raised with Him, we become co-heirs of an inheritance alongside Jesus. And we have the Holy Spirit as a guarantee of that inheritance. When we put on the new man, we activate Jesus' offer to live His life through us. Our old self has been done away with, and we become new creations. By receiving the "righteousness in Him" that His death achieved for us, we have been reconciled to God, and we become agents of reconciliation on His behalf.

Now reconciled to God, we embrace the role of reconciling others to God which Paul calls being ambassadors We must recognize that we have been reconciled, and so become His agents of reconciliation. We also get to discover the loving trust our Creator and Redeemer places in us to do what He purposed for us to do on His earth. Embracing His purpose and His power is necessary for our "Eden" inheritance to be restored. Think of the two concepts—restoration and reconciliation—in relational context. In order for a relationship to be restored, it must be reconciled. The cause of the breach or offense must be accounted for and removed in order for the relationship to be restored. The same is true in our relationship with God. Jesus' death and resurrection justify us before the Father, wiping clear the offense of our sin against our holy God. Then the path is cleared for us to be restored to the Father's inheritance.

Living in Light of Our New Identity

As we examined in Galatians and Ephesians, Paul describes how the death and resurrection of Jesus achieves this reconciliation with God. We are reconciled by His blood and receive His righteousness.[382] To experience the nature of life God provided Adam and Eve, this reconciliation is required. Paul says God makes us a new creation by which we receive one of His most important gifts.

"For the love of Christ controls us, having concluded this, that one died for all, therefore all died; and He died for all, so that they who live might no longer live for themselves, but for Him who died and rose again on their behalf...Therefore if anyone is in Christ, *he is* a new creature; the old things passed away; behold, new things have come. Now all *these* things are from God, who reconciled us to Himself through Christ and gave us the ministry of reconciliation, namely, that God was in Christ reconciling the world to Himself, not counting their trespasses against them, and He has committed to us the word of reconciliation. Therefore, we are ambassadors for Christ, as though God were making an appeal through us; we beg you on behalf of Christ, be reconciled to God. He made Him who knew no sin *to be* sin on our behalf, so that we might become the righteousness of God in Him." (2 Corinthians 5:14-21 NAS 1995)[383]

Hopefully one of the messages you have taken from this book is this: Please don't live for yourself! God has a much better purpose for you than you could dream for yourself or achieve in your own strength. Each of our stories has a much better ending than we could ever have imagined! Instead of living for self, we should persevere in our faith and become overcomers. The question is not whether we are a "Christian" in name, for Jesus said there would be those who name His name but whom He never knew. Instead, we receive His promises when we persevere in our faith, even in the midst of suffering.[384] When we maintain our testimony as His followers, He considers us an overcomer. We will see the importance of this identity in the book of Revelation.[385]

Eden Is for Overcomers: Jesus and His Victory

Earlier in this book, we saw that not only does Jesus win the victory over Satan and make a display of that victory to the heavenly witnesses, but the Father gives us that victory Jesus earned over Satan and death![386] Jesus won the victory, and because He is in us, we get the benefit of that victory!

Because "victory" and "victorious" are often translated as "overcome," it is possible to undervalue what that victory means. We know people who have overcome various obstacles, pains, or losses in their life, and though we may applaud their perseverance and courage, that "overcoming" story means more to them than it does to us. But in the instance of Jesus' victory, though it did bring Him joy as He rescued for Himself a bride, that victory has everything to do with our present and future, and it erases the penalty of our past. So just how does His victory make us overcomers?

Overcomers Face Hardship with Confidence

There will certainly be hardships present in our lives until the day Jesus returns. But the apostle John says that all who endure, those who overcome, will experience the promised redemption. As we read in Revelation, there are three realities that mark people as overcomers. First, the blood of the Lamb, Jesus, has cleansed their sin. Another is their testimony of faith in Jesus who is at work in them for His purposes. The third reality is that they maintain their testimony in the face of suffering, even unto death. John says,

> "Then I heard a loud voice in heaven, saying, 'Now the salvation, and the power, and the kingdom of our God and the authority of His Christ have come, for the accuser of our brethren has been thrown down, he who accuses them before our God day and night. And they overcame him because of the blood of the Lamb and because of the word of their testimony, and they did not love their life even when faced with death.'" (Revelation 12:10-11 NAS 1995) [387]

If you have already died and your life is hidden with Christ in God, then facing physical death is no problem! You don't count your life as precious to yourself. Paul, having told the Galatians that we must be crucified with Jesus, understood the mindset John proclaims. He expressed the same to the Ephesian elders in Acts 20 clearly. Paul believed his life on earth to be of value only as it served his mission, to share the gospel of grace.

> "But I do not consider my life of any account as dear to myself, so that I may finish my course and the ministry which I received from the Lord Jesus, to testify solemnly of the gospel of the grace of God."[388]

In Acts 27, he also expresses confidence that God will fulfill His purpose for him. In this section of Scripture, Paul was on his way to Rome by ship. It says "The severe storm kept raging. Finally all hope that we would be saved was disappearing." (Acts 27:20 HCS)[389] With the storm coming against them, Paul speaks up.

> "Now listen to me. Don't be depressed, for no one will perish-only the ship will be lost. For God's angel visited me last night, the angel of my God, the God I passionately serve. He came and stood in front of me and said, 'Don't be afraid, Paul. You are destined to stand trial before Caesar. And because of God's favor on you, he has given you the lives of everyone who is sailing with you.' So men, keep up your courage! I know that God will protect you, just as he told me he would." (Acts 27:22-25 TPT)[390]

Paul knew that the angel who appeared to him was sent from God and that the situation would unfold just as God said. He told those on the ship to take courage. We can conclude that Paul was facing a fearful situation before the angel's appearance. Why would the angel say, "Don't be afraid, Paul," unless the situation warranted that feeling? But once he heard what God intended to happen, Paul had confidence in God, and courage to face the situation. After all, he said I do not "consider my life of any account as dear to myself, so that I may finish my course and the ministry which I received."[391] He had already died to himself, and knew that his life was directed, protected, and empowered by Jesus working through him. He was not bound to a mindset that forced him into fearing a shipwreck. He had confidence in the fact he had heard from God that all would be safe among the ship's passengers. And Paul persisted in that confidence even when verbally challenged by passengers who failed to believe. He displayed this confidence when threatened by a snakebite that those around him assumed would be deadly. Paul shook the snake off and suffered no harm.[392] When time passed and he did not die, those on ship actually thought he was a god. The reality is that he received a word of assurance sent by God through an angel that he would survive. No snake was going to get in the way of God fulfilling His word. Instead, Paul ministered to Publius' father on the island of Malta where they came ashore. Through Paul's prayer, the man was healed. Paul overcame his own fear by the promise of God. When we understand our inheritance, we too can overcome fear. Hearing and obeying God fulfills His will in situations where we face fear.

Overcomers believe Jesus won the victory over the world, death, and fear. They belong to the family of God by virtue of this belief. Overcomers inherit God's promise to His children of the new heaven and new earth. To display the courage of an overcomer, it is essential to respond to God from a position of faith and not fear. The fate of those who don't exercise courage and faith is serious.

How Seriously God Takes Fear: The Fate of the Unbelieving

John is clear in Revelation 21 about those who fail to believe and therefore overcome. They will experience eternal death.

> And He who sits on the throne said, "Behold, I am making all things new." And He said, "Write, for these words are faithful and true." Then He said to me, "It is done. I am the Alpha and the Omega, the beginning and the end. I will give to the one who thirsts from the spring of the water of life without cost. "He who overcomes will inherit these things, and I will be his God and he will be My son. "But for the cowardly and unbelieving and abominable and murderers and immoral persons and sorcerers and idolaters and all liars, their part *will be* in the lake that burns with fire and brimstone, which is the second death." (Revelation 21:5-8, NAS 1995)[393]

By overcoming, God says we are His sons and daughters. We will experience the satisfaction of our thirst from a spring containing living water. But if we embrace fear and doubt instead of being an overcomer, we will be judged. Paul says God has not given us the spirit of fear (cowardice); but of power, and of love, and of a sound mind.[394] Since a spirit of cowardice is not from God, it must originate from the enemy of our souls, to entice us to disbelieve the purpose we were made for. Fear takes root in the flesh and causes us to shrink back, to doubt His goodness or doubt His will. Though we may have instances where we fear, rather than living in fear (terror) of God, there should be an awe of what God has done and is doing that drives us forward in our faith and our fellowship with Him.

We see in Acts that with proper awe of God and an acceptance of the work of the Comforter, the Holy Spirit, the early church grew. "So the church throughout all Judea and Galilee and Samaria enjoyed peace, being built up; and going on in the fear of the Lord and in the comfort of the Holy Spirit, it continued to increase." (Acts 9:31, NAS1995)[395]

Our choice is to believe God is who He says He is, and therefore we are who He says we are: sons and daughters of His household. With holy awe for what we have received, we strive to be overcomers. Banishing the negative fear of Him, we can stand in awe of what He has done and rejoice in it.

The Picture of Eden Restored

I began the argument for being "Made for Eden" with the creation and fall of mankind accounts, then focused on Jesus' and Paul's understanding of Eden as our reality and its promises for our destiny. God chooses to end His written Word to mankind with John's visions. In the last chapter of the Bible, Revelation 22, we see the existence of mankind come full circle. What Adam and Eve lost, mankind now regains. What we were made for is again ours by right of inheritance, given to all the overcomers.

A friend kindly gave me a wonderful book on the feasts of the Lord given to Israel. There is so much symbolism of spiritual reality in the feasts Israel observed. The book's title suggests that what God began to do through symbols, He will complete in reality. The day is coming when all the pictures will be restored.[396] Paul says of Adam being a picture of the coming Redeemer, "Adam, who is a type of Him who was to come."[397] Jesus was the second Adam, the One whose grace flowed to many.

Pictures remind us of pleasant times past. How often do you see an image that stirs joy or love in you? For me, I am grateful for a large camera roll! I can go back years and find images of places I have enjoyed in the Father's created world, of a sunset or a mountain. Also, pictures of my family bring certain memories back in an instant. Each of these images reminds me of His love.

At the end of the Bible, I can picture the scene in my mind's eye, especially the tree described. This lengthy quotation from Revelation 22 describes this paradise regained in the New Jerusalem.

"Then he showed me a river of the water of life, clear as crystal, coming from the throne of God and of the Lamb, in the middle of its street. On either side of the river was the tree of life, bearing twelve *kinds of* fruit, yielding its fruit every month; and the leaves of the tree were for the healing of the nations. There will no longer be any curse; and the throne of God and of the Lamb will be in it, and His bond-servants will serve Him; they will see His face, and His name *will be* on their foreheads. And there will no longer be *any* night; and they will not have need of the light of a lamp nor the light of the sun, because the Lord God will illumine them; and they will reign forever and ever. And he said to me, 'These words are faithful and true; and the Lord, the God of the spirits of the prophets, sent His angel to show to His bond-servants the things which must soon take place. And behold, I am coming quickly. Blessed is he who heeds the words of the prophecy of this book'... 'Behold, I am coming quickly, and My reward *is* with Me, to render to every man according to what he has done. I am the Alpha and the Omega, the first and the last, the beginning and the end. Blessed are those who wash their robes, so that they may have the right to the tree of life, and may enter by the gates into the city' ... Spirit and the bride say, 'Come.' And let the one who hears say, 'Come.' And let the one who is thirsty come; let the one who wishes take the water of life without cost. I testify to everyone who hears the words of the prophecy of this book: if anyone adds to them, God will add to him the plagues which are written in this book; and if anyone takes away from the words of the book of this prophecy, God will take away his part from the tree of life and from the holy city, which are written in this book." (Revelation 22:1-7, 12-19 NAS 1995)[398]

This final chapter of the Bible is rich with promises, and being God's final written revelation, contains keys for understanding the Eden we were made for. The first parallel with the original creation in Genesis is the presence of the tree of life.

Revelation 22:2 says, "On either side of the river was the tree of life, bearing twelve kinds of fruit, yielding its fruit every month ..." (NAS1995)[399] This tree of life may be a re-creation of the original.[400] It is found on either side of the river, either as two trees or perhaps one large enough to stretch over the river.

Even before Jesus identified Himself as the source of life, we have a picture of the future source of life in Ezekiel 47, which says there is a river that flows from the house of God which brings life and healing.[401] The Hebrew term for "house" is consistent with usage elsewhere for God's house.[402] So in Revelation 22, the river flowing from the throne is the same as Ezekiel 47 where it flows from the house, or temple. The Godhead dwells on the throne, life flows from the throne. At the end of time, this throne is the ruling center of the kingdom, and is the most important element of the New Eden.

It is prophesied in Ezekiel 47:12: "By the river on its bank, on one side and on the other, will grow all *kinds of* trees for food. Their leaves will not wither and their fruit will not fail. They will bear every month because their water flows from the sanctuary, and their fruit will be for food and their leaves for healing." This is fulfilled in Revelation 22:2. "… the tree of life, bearing twelve *kinds of* fruit, yielding its fruit every month; and the leaves of the tree were for the healing of the nations." So its leaves contain healing properties, just as Ezekiel prophesied.

The Final Beatitude

The final proclamation of the Bible, what has been called the Final Beatitude of Jesus, is that those who wear their robe, one that has been cleansed by Jesus' blood, have the right to the tree of life!

> "Blessed are those who wash their robes, so that they may have the right to the tree of life, and may enter by the gates into the city."[403]

The blood of Jesus is the only thing that can cleanse our garments that were made filthy by sin and make us worthy of the identity the Father has given us.[404] The renewed access to the Tree of Life is for those who have washed their robes. That is, they are made clean by the blood of the Savior. This is a promise of the reversal of the judgment upon Adam and Eve, who were barred from the garden and from the Tree of Life after their sin. God stations cherubim with swords at the edge of the garden, to prevent Adam and Eve from eating of the Tree of Life.[405] We are told that the Tree of Life was in the middle of the Garden of Eden, and Revelation 22 tells us it is prominent in the New Jerusalem.

Curse Reversed: A Tree and A Robe to Overcomers

Even before the final scene of Scripture announces the restoration of mankind's access to the Tree of Life, and the importance of cleansed robes, these concepts are interwoven earlier in Revelation. Revelation 2 says, "He who has an ear, let him hear what the Spirit says to the churches. To him who overcomes, I will grant to eat of the tree of life which is in the Paradise of God."[406] And Revelation 3:4–5 says "But you have a few people in Sardis who have not soiled their garments; and they will walk with Me in white, for they are worthy. He who overcomes will thus be clothed in white garments; and I will not erase his name from the book of life, and I will confess his name before My Father and before His angels."[407]

Not only do overcomers have access to the Tree of Life as existed in Eden, but we will also walk with Jesus, dressed in white. We will be walking in His victory. The post-sin realities of pain, loss, sorrow will be no more. The vision in Revelation 7, of God providing the water of life to those who thirst, and of wiping away tears from their eyes, is reinforced in Revelation 21.

"And I saw the holy city, New Jerusalem, coming down out of heaven from God, made ready as a bride adorned for her husband. And I heard a loud voice from the throne, saying, 'Behold, the tabernacle of God is among men, and He will dwell among them, and they shall be His people, and God Himself will be among them, and He will wipe away every tear from their eyes; and there will no longer be *any* death; there will no longer be *any* mourning, or crying, or pain; the first things have passed away.' And He who sits on the throne said, 'Behold, I am making all things new.' And He said, 'Write, for these words are faithful and true.' Then He said to me, 'It is done. I am the Alpha and the Omega, the beginning and the end. I will give to the one who thirsts from the spring of the water of life without cost. He who overcomes will inherit these things, and I will be his God and he will be My son.'" (Revelation 21:2-7 NAS 1995)[408]

Then once more, returning to Revelation 22:17 says,

"The Spirit and the bride say, 'Come.' And let the one who hears say, 'Come.' And let the one who is thirsty come; let the one who wishes take the water of life without cost." (NAS 1995)[409]

The Lamb will guide the faithful to the living waters. And as God's sons, He gives us life, represented by the water, as a gift. This seems to follow the description in Ezekiel 47:9, that everything will live where the river goes.

The setting that Adam and Eve dwelt among—rivers and a Tree of Life—from which they were shut off after their sin, becomes the dwelling place of the redeemed. This place will be revealed when the new Jerusalem comes down out of heaven. Those who wash their robes (are cleansed by the shedding of Jesus' blood) therefore have the right to the Tree of Life once again. What was lost was not lost forever but was regained through the sacrifice of Jesus for sin, by which He defeated the devil and took back dominion over the earth.

Creation, and mankind, will be fully redeemed at the coming and final return of the Redeemer, Jesus, which He says is quickly approaching.[410]

As we said about the cowardly and unbelieving in Revelation 21:8, so here God says what would prevent someone their access to the Tree of Life or the New Jerusalem is taking away from the words of the book of this prophecy. The integrity of our belief in His message to us about our destiny is of utmost importance to our Father. We must understand our reconciliation to God, and "the restoration of all things," in order to know beyond a shadow of doubt His nature as provider and redeemer.

It is remarkable that the last page of the book of Revelation should reflect the first pages of Genesis. The period of human history just after Adam and Eve's sin began with cherubim bearing flaming swords barring the way to the Tree of Life. In the New Heaven and New Earth, the cherubim guarding the Tree of Life are no longer given that task. Perhaps those same cherubim, instead of guarding the forbidden tree, prohibiting entrance, may be present at the tree, inviting us to taste of what Jesus has restored to us. The fact that the Bible begins and ends with a tree may be God's way of saying that all that falls between these periods of history, all death and hardship, is a reminder that God's purpose will prevail no matter the actions of mankind. That's why being Made for Eden is such a life changing truth! The glorious restoration of God's people to the environment He created them for is revealed to all mankind. Not only were we Made for Eden, we get to experience it again!

May you drink deeply of His promised future for you, a future sealed for all who overcome. May it strengthen your walk as His new creation, now and until His return.

EPILOGUE

What's Next?

My final two chapters were an attempt to demonstrate the context for the fulfillment of our restoration to Eden. Despite the hardship that Paul says is inevitable for believers in the last days, the description of a believer's life, empowered by God and made effective for the purposes of God, remains true. The presence of sin, evil, and suffering does not negate what we were made for. And the renewed access to the "environment of God," whether in the Garden in Eden or the New Jerusalem, depends on the washing we receive from Jesus' sacrifice of Himself.

A commitment to applying this truth of being made for Eden was my primary goal. If I were simply restating universally accepted truth among the Body of Christ, there would be a very small "takeaway" from this book. But I believe Paul learned the importance of the message he was to spread among the gentiles while under the illumination of Holy Spirit in Arabia. His understanding of what Jesus had accomplished by His death and resurrection was planted deep within his spirit during the years after God appeared to him while on the Damascus Road. And this vitally important message for God's people is that we were made for relationship with God, who paved the way for our return to relationship. The truth that He is renewing us to His original intent has not been fully assimilated into the gospel many of Christ's disciples proclaim in the twentieth century. I believe there is a new "call to arms" to be issued.

George MacDonald, as quoted in the last chapter, says "All the growth of the Christian is the more and more life he is receiving."[411] In far too many discussions of what Jesus came to do, the conclusion within Christian circles is that His main goal is to save us from sin's penalty and allow us into heaven. But Jesus said that His appearance on earth is meant to give us life, and to undo the devil's work.[412] He also said to His disciples that following Him to receive that life would involve sacrifice and obedience. "If anyone wishes to come after Me, he must deny himself, and take up his cross and follow Me. For whoever wishes to save his life will lose it; but whoever loses his life for My sake will find it. For what will it profit a man if he gains the whole world and forfeits his soul? Or what will a man give in exchange for his soul? For the Son of Man is going to come in the glory of His Father with His angels, and then will repay every man according to his deeds." (Matthew 16:24-27)[413]

What we need is not to *make more happen through our life*, but rather, we need more *life*, so we can be involved in the Father's business until He returns. It is our privilege to use the talents He has entrusted to us "with interest," that is, showing a return on what He gave us. We are to make every effort to honor the call of being His ambassadors. Both Peter and Paul urge the adding of qualities to our life that make us *more effective* in that calling.

"For this very reason, make every effort to supplement your faith with virtue, and virtue with knowledge, and knowledge with self-control, and self-control with steadfastness, and steadfastness with godliness, and godliness with brotherly affection, and brotherly affection with love. For if these qualities are yours and are increasing, they keep you from being ineffective or unfruitful in the knowledge of our Lord Jesus Christ. (1 Peter 1:5-8 ESV)[414]

Peter is saying that by growing in these qualities, it keeps you from being ineffective or unfruitful in the true knowledge of Jesus. The word for ineffective is literally "idle or useless," even lazy. And unfruitful is literally without fruit. We are to make every effort toward virtue and self-control, to being diligent and persevering, and above all, to love. Having these qualities regularly exhibited in us accelerates the process of our renewal into the Eden life, since it keeps you from being ineffective or unfruitful in Jesus. If we compare this verse to Colossians 3:9-10, Paul says the new man, the identity we receive in Christ, *is* being renewed in this true knowledge.

> "Do not lie to one another, since you laid aside the old self with its *evil* practices, and have put on the new self who is being renewed to a true knowledge according to the image of the One who created him." (Colossians 3:9-10 NAS 1995)[415]

Taking these passages together, we can say that when we make every effort to have godly qualities shine through us, by the power of Christ in me, we are strengthening the new man. We are operating according to the image we were made in, the image of our Creator.[416]

Paul also states something else to strive toward. "Make every effort to keep the unity of the Spirit through the bond of peace." (Ephesians 4:3 NIV)[417] We are to strive for unity in the One Spirit and one faith that we are part of.[418]

In the next to last chapter, I argued for giving God's Word and God's Spirit full reign over our walk and our thoughts and full honor in our actions. To prepare the ground of our heart and plant the right seeds in it to produce a harvest of Eden life, we should do several things.

Present Ourselves to God as an Act of Worship

The first thing we must do is to consider our lives as a sacrifice unto God. By presenting ourselves to Him, we accept His purpose for our lives, and take our role as a steward to a higher level. Paul says, "Therefore I urge you, brothers and sisters, by the mercies of God, to present your bodies as a living and holy sacrifice, acceptable to God, which is your spiritual service of worship."[419]

Prepare Ourselves for His Revelation at the Time Known Only to the Father

We should live as those who are bought for God by the powerful sacrifice of Jesus of His blood which cleanses us from our past. And we should live as though the return of Jesus is near, being prepared to act by His direction, and being sober in our purpose. Peter says, "Therefore, prepare your minds for action, keep sober *in spirit,* fix your hope completely on the grace to be brought to you at the revelation of Jesus Christ. As obedient children, do not be conformed to the former lusts *which were yours* in your ignorance, but like the Holy One who called you, be holy yourselves also in all *your* behavior; because it is written, 'You shall be holy, for I am holy.' ... knowing that you were not redeemed with perishable things like silver or gold from your futile way of life inherited from your forefathers, but with precious blood, as of a lamb unblemished and spotless, *the blood* of Christ." (1 Peter 1:13-19 NAS1995)[420]

Assure Ourselves of the Benefit of Abiding in Him

Abiding in Jesus means we depend on His life-giving presence and direction daily. We are a branch drawing its very life from the vine. Doing this assures us that we will be ready for His return. John says, "This is the promise which He Himself made to us: eternal life. These things I have written to you concerning those who are trying to deceive you. As for you, the anointing which you received from Him abides in you, and you have no need for anyone to teach you; but as His anointing teaches you about all things, and is true and is not a lie, and just as it has taught you, you abide in Him. Now, little children, abide in Him, so that when He appears, we may have confidence and not shrink away from Him in shame at His coming." (1 John 2:25-28 NAS 1995)[421]

Comfort Ourselves with the Certain Result of Persevering in Faith

There is comfort in keeping ourselves in the love of Jesus. Those who maintain their commitment to Jesus are marked as overcomers and will be forever in His presence. Jesus, through a vision of John, says,

"Behold, I have put before you an open door which no one can shut, because you have a little power, and have kept My word, and have not denied My name … The one who overcomes, I will make him a pillar in the temple of My God, and he will not go out from it anymore; and I will write on him the name of My God, and the name of the city of My God, the new Jerusalem, which comes down out of heaven from My God, and

My new name. 'The one who has an ear, let him hear what the Spirit says to the churches.'"[422]

If we hear what the Spirit says, we can have the hope which will sustain us until the end of our time on earth.

Paul says that the message he proclaims about Jesus is the mystery of all ages revealed and, by us embracing it, God will establish us as His own, ready to do what He created us for. "Now to Him who is able to establish you according to my gospel and the preaching of Jesus Christ, according to the revelation of the mystery which has been kept secret for long ages past, but now is manifested, and by the Scriptures of the prophets, according to the commandment of the eternal God, has been made known to all the nations, leading to obedience of faith; to the only wise God, through Jesus Christ, be the glory forever. Amen." (Romans 16:25-27 NAS 1995) [423]

Finally, after He establishes us as His own, we will be blameless and joyful as we encounter Him and stand in His presence. "Now to Him who is able to protect you from stumbling, and to make you stand in the presence of His glory blameless with great joy, to the only God our Savior, through Jesus Christ our Lord, be glory, majesty, dominion and authority, before all time and now and forever. Amen."[424]

Come, Lord Jesus. May we be ready for your return, as You usher in the next phase of Your kingdom and bring us into Eden in New Jerusalem on the new earth.

Endnotes

1 Genesis 1:26.

2 Matthew 6:10.

3 Ephesians 1:3, 3:20.

4 He who has the Son has life. 1 John 5:11.

5 Jesus shows this is something we pray for, in His prayer in Matthew 6:10.

6 Exodus 19:5–6.

7 1 Peter 1:1–2 "aliens, who are chosen according to the foreknowledge of God the Father, by the sanctifying work of the Spirit, to obey Jesus Christ and be sprinkled with His blood." (NAS 1995)
1 Peter 1:17–21 ...conduct yourselves in fear during the time of your stay *on earth;* knowing that you were not redeemed with perishable things like silver or gold from your futile way of life inherited from your forefathers, but with precious blood, as of a lamb unblemished and spotless, *the blood* of Christ. (NAS 1995)

8 1 Corinthians 3:23 ...you belong to Christ; and Christ belongs to God. And 1 Corinthians 6:18–20 But the one who joins himself to the Lord is one spirit *with Him...* For you have been bought with a price: therefore glorify God in your body.

9 Romans 12:1.

10 See Colossians 1:15–17. "He is the image of the invisible God, the firstborn of all creation. For by Him all things were created...all things have been created through Him and for Him. He is before all things, and in Him all things hold together."

11 Lewis, C.S. The Complete CS Lewis Signature Classics, San Francisco, HarperOne, 2007, 113.

12 Ibid.

13 Ibid, 114.

14 Ibid.

15 Ecclesiastes 3:11 tells us He set eternity in our hearts. This desire for the heavenly will either seek fulfillment in eternal or perishable things.
2 Peter 1:4

16 Sinless existence in Genesis 1:31, 2:25, and again without sin in the end (1 Corinthians 6:9, Revelation 21:4, 22:3,15).

[17] Ephesians 2:10.

[18] Read again anew Psalms 139:16. "in Your book were written all the days that were ordained *for me*, when as yet there was not one of them."

[19] Colossians 1:20, The Passion Translation.

[20] Matthew 1:21.

[21] Matthew 3:11, 17.

[22] Exodus 34:29. See 2 Corinthians 3:18 about the faces of the redeemed.

[23] Acts 2:38. Peter says "Repent, and each of you be baptized in the name of Jesus Christ for the forgiveness of your sins, and you will receive the gift of the Holy Spirit."

[24] Matthew 27:5.

[25] Isaiah 30:21.

[26] John 10:27.

[27] See Ezekiel 28:14. God placed him in the Garden of Eden.

[28] Luke 24:26–27.

[29] John 14:15–21, 23.

[30] Luke 11:36.

[31] Hebrews 1:3.

[32] 1 Peter 1:3–4.

[33] Ephesians 1:3,6, Philippians 4:19.

[34] Genesis 1:26–28.

[35] Genesis 2:8–10.

[36] Genesis 2:15.

[37] Jesus, He whose name is above every name, gives us a new name as a victor or overcomes, according to Revelation 3:12. He also calls us friends in John 15:15. What God calls something gives it its highest purpose.

[38] For more explanation of the term in medieval times, see "Steward (office)." *Wikipedia*, Wikimedia Foundation, 23 Apr. 2021, en.wikipedia.org/wiki/Steward_(office).

[39] https://firstrate.com/blog/becoming-a-wealth-steward-in-five-steps

[40] Genesis 39:8.

[41] Matthew 25:21.

[42] Luke 16:1–2, 8, 12 (HCS). For another discussion, one should consider Luke 17:5–10. Jesus encourages us to see ourselves as unworthy (KJV unprofitable) servants as we do what is commanded.

But the context is of expecting obstacles in our way to obey us, when we speak with authority.

43 Titus 1:7.

44 Luke 12:48. (NKJV).

45 2 Timothy 2:15.

46 We are literally His poiema, a work of His creativity. We get the English word "poem" from this Greek term. He fashions us, as a writer does a poem.

47 Genesis 3:17–19.

48 Revelation 5:9–10.

49 2 Peter 3:13 (context is verses 11–18) says that the coming of the new heaven and new earth should prompt us to grow in the grace and knowledge of our Lord.

50 Genesis 3:10.

51 Matthew 19:28, Acts 3:21

52 Romans 8:19–22.

53 Genesis 1:26 (ESV). See also Genesis 1:28 on rule or dominion.

54 Romans 1:20. "For since the creation of the world His invisible attributes, His eternal power and divine nature, have been clearly seen, being understood through what has been made, so that they are without excuse." NAS 1995.

55 Ephesians 2:12.

56 Exodus 33:19–23.

57 Exodus 34:29–30.

58 Exodus 33:9–11.

59 Galatians 4:4.

60 Isaiah 55:8.

61 1 Corinthians 1:27.

62 1 Samuel 16:3–13 and Exodus 3:4, 4:10–19.

63 Romans 1:7, 1 Cor 1:2.

64 1 Corinthians 1:27–30 (TPT). See also Matthew 20:6, the first will end up last and the last will end up being first.

65 See also Matthew 19:16–30, Mark 10:17–31 and Luke 18:18–30. The rich man was told to give to the poor, to show that God's truth had taken hold in his heart, and therefor had not neglected mercy and generosity while keeping other commands.

66 Genesis 2:8–9.

67 Genesis 2:15–17.

[68] Genesis 3:1–5. (NKJV)

[69] They were made in His image, or likeness, according to Genesis 1:27.

[70] Genesis 3:22–24.

[71] Genesis 3:7, 12, 13.

[72] Matthew 25:24–27.

[73] 2 Corinthians 3:12–16.

[74] 2 Corinthians 4:3–4.

[75] 2 Corinthians 10:4–5 (NAS 1995).

[76] Colossians 1:13.

[77] Ephesians 2:11–16 is full text.

[78] God said, "cursed is the ground, in toil you will eat of it." Genesis 3:17 (NAS 1995).

[79] Genesis 6:5-9 (NAS 1995).

[80] Revelation 5:9.

[81] Revelation 13:8.

[82] Our role as kings and priests is established, according to Revelation 1:5–6, 5:10.

[83] Matthew 10:39, 16:25.

[84] Ephesians 5:1.

[85] Ephesians 1:3–5, 13–14.

[86] Acts 11:26.

[87] Acts 14:12–18

[88] 1 Corinthians 1:13. Here, Paul asks the Corinthians, who were dividing themselves between who they followed, he asks "Is Christ divided?" When you say, "I am of Paul," or "I am of Cephas, or with Apollos, are you not elevating a man?" Paul wants to ensure that they are clear on who brought them into God's family. "Was it Paul who was crucified for you? Or were you baptized in Paul's name?"

[89] Lewis stresses how important the life of Christ in us is to living out our faith. "What I want to make clear is that this (putting on Christ) is not one among many jobs a Christian has to do; and *it is not a sort of exercise for the top class. It is the whole of Christianity.*" Lewis, C.S. The Complete CS Lewis Signature Classics, p.156.

[90] Matthew 16:24, 25, Matthew 7:14.

[91] Ibid, 156.

[92] Ibid, 158.

[93] Ibid, 157.

94 See Romans 7:18. Also Jesus in John 6:62 says the Spirit gives life, the flesh profits nothing.

95 See Galatians 5:16–18, also Romans 8. Following Spirit enables you to live above the desires of the flesh.

96 Romans 8:6–8

97 Lewis, C.S. The Complete CS Lewis Signature Classics, p 158.

98 Matthew 6:24.

99 Paul says with the heart man believes, and that our minds must be renewed. See Romans, chapters 10 and 12.

100 Matthew 23:25, Luke 11:39

101 Romans 8:2

102 1 Corinthians 15:55–57, Luke 20:36. See also 2 Timothy 1:10, Revelation 1:18.

103 Hebrews 2:14

104 Lewis, C.S. The Complete CS Lewis Signature Classics, p 159.

105 A fuller study of the church as Christ's Bride is well worth the study. Jesus eventually celebrates a marriage supper with, having purchased or redeemed her for Himself.

106 Ibid, 161.

107 James 1:4. We must let patience, or endurance, have its result, perfection.

108 Lewis, C.S. The Complete CS Lewis Signature Classics, p. 161.

109 Lewis says, "no power in the whole universe, except you yourself, can prevent Him from taking you to that goal. That is what you are in for." Ibid, 161.

110 Ibid, 162.

111 Matthew 7:7–11, Philippians 4:19.

112 Romans 12:3.

113 Revelation 21:8, 2 Timothy 1:7.

114 Philippians 1:6, "For I am confident of this very thing, that He who began a good work in you will perfect it until the day of Christ Jesus."

115 Ibid, 163.

116 2 Timothy 2:21.

117 See Matthew 5:45.

118 Matthew 5:48.

119 Ibid, 170.

120 Ephesians 2:10.

121 Matthew 16:25 (TPT).

122 1 Peter 2:21.

123 One such example would be Peter cutting off Malchus' ear and telling Jesus he was wrong to choose the path of the cross.

124 Matthew 23:23.

125 Matthew 23:25.

126 Matthew 23:28.

127 Matthew 3:17.

128 Matthew 17:5.

129 John 4:34 "My food is to do the will of Him who sent Me, and to accomplish His work." John 6:38 says "I have come down from heaven not to do My own will, but the will of Him who sent Me."

130 Matthew 4:4 and Luke 4:4 say, "Man shall not live on bread alone, but on every Word (spoken word) that comes out of the mouth of God."

131 John 10:17–18 (NAS 1995).

132 John 13:3 (HCS).

133 Philippians 2:3–11.

134 John 11:1–8.

135 John 11:11–15. In the Greek, the word for death is clear. Lazarus is separate from life, dead.

136 John 11:21–26.

137 John 11:32–35.

138 In verse 14, Jesus says "Lazarus is dead" before He has seen Him. He must have discerned this fact by God's Spirit, we are not told that someone came from Lazarus' house to inform Jesus.

139 The Jewish belief that the soul remained near the body for days after the death, guarded by shomrim, is interesting for noting their view of death. See "Shemira." *Wikipedia*, Wikimedia Foundation, 23 Apr. 2021, en.wikipedia.org/wiki/Shemira.

140 John 11:41–43.

141 Jesus tells his disciples to do the same in Matthew 10:8, for "freely you received, freely give."

142 John 8:28–29.

143 John 11:42.

144 From John 5:19. There are many statements in the Gospels about what Jesus came to bring, and they all stem from the Father's purpose for mankind. He came that we may have abundant life, John 10:10.

He came to make his home in us, John 14:23. He lived to serve, Matthew 10:28. He goes to prepare a place for us, that we may be with Him where He is, John 14:3. He came that we may be in unity with the Trinity, John 17:21.

145 Philippians 2:7.

146 Luke 17:6–10.

147 Mark 9:23, 11:23-24, 16:17.

148 These include NKJV, KJV, ESV, NIV. HCS, NLT.

149 Matthew 25:23.

150 See Matthew 25:24–30.

151 Galatians 2:20.

152 Matthew 7:11.

153 Matthew 25:23.

154 Matthew 3:2, 4:17.

155 Eldredge, John. Journey of Desire. Thomas Nelson, 2000. P. 113.

156 1 John 5:19.

157 Matthew 4:23–24.

158 Luke 18:29–30.

159 James 1:12, "A man who endures trials is blessed, because when he passes the test he will receive the crown of life that God has promised to those who love Him." And 2 Timothy 4:8 "There is reserved for me in the future the crown of righteousness, which the Lord, the righteous Judge, will give me on that day, and not only to me, but to all those who have loved His appearing."

160 John 5:19b–20.

161 John 15:15.

162 John 14:10, Colossians 1:29, Philippians 2:13.

163 John 14:30–31. The expression in Greek is a double negative. Jesus says Satan literally "has not nothing" in Him.

164 1 Peter 2:21–23. Read 1 Peter 2:19–25 in The Passion Translation on the Cross and dying to sin.

165 Matthew 16:24–25.

166 Acts 9:20.

167 Acts 10:38, 1 Corinthians 15:3, Romans 3:25, Ephesians 1:7

168 Philippians 3:4–6.

169 Philippians 3:3.

[170] Galatians 2:20. This book speaks about false views of how to become righteous and is a strong defense of how life in Christ relates to Law.

[171] Galatians 2:20 (TPT).

[172] The Message Bible translates Galatians 2:20 this way. "I am no longer driven to impress God. Christ lives in me. The life you see me living is not 'mine' but it is lived by faith in the Son of God, who loved me and gave himself for me … If a *living relationship with God* could come by rule-keeping, then Christ died unnecessarily." (MSG)

[173] John 12:24–25.

[174] Matthew 11:28–30. (HCS)

[175] Galatians 2:15–16 (MSG).

[176] Romans 6:4.

[177] Paul uses an analogy from marriage in Romans 7 to reinforce this freedom from the law.

[178] Romans 6:23 For the wages of sin is death, but the free gift of God is eternal life in Christ Jesus our Lord.

[179] Romans 6:6–7. Romans 6:1–11 expand the theme of these verses.

[180] Philippians 3:10, The Passion Translation.

[181] David Wilkerson, I am Not Mad at God, Minneapolis, Bethany Fellowship, 1967, p.24. He was founding pastor at Times Square Church in New York City, and known for his book The Cross and the Switchblade.

[182] Ibid, 24.

[183] Ibid, 25.

[184] Romans 8:11 (TPT).

[185] Colossians 1:28-29 (TPT).

[186] Romans 8:1 (TPT).

[187] David Wilkerson, I am Not Mad at God, Minneapolis, Bethany Fellowship, 1967, p.26.

[188] Galatians 2:20.

[189] Romans 6:10–11 (TPT).

[190] See Hebrews 12:4 on resisting sin intently.

[191] 2 Corinthians 11:24–28 (NAS 1995).

[192] 2 Corinthians 10:17.

[193] Colossians 3:1–4.

[194] Romans 6:6,17.

[195] Philippians 4:8 (TPT).

[196] Ephesians 4:24 (HCS).

[197] Ephesians 4:24 (TPT).

[198] Romans 13:14.

[199] Platt, David. Something Needs to Change. Colorado Springs: Multnomah, 2019, p. 116.

[200] "Audience with the King," August 17 reading. Cowman, L.B. Streams in the Desert. Grand Rapids, Zondervan, 1996.

[201] Philippians 2:13–16.

[202] Philippians 3:7–8.

[203] 2 Corinthians 5:21.

[204] Philippians 3:10.

[205] Lewis says, "other men become 'new' by being 'in Him.'" In other words, the new creation is defined as one that is "in Christ." Lewis, The Complete CS Lewis, 173.

[206] Lewis, The Complete CS Lewis, 59.

[207] Ibid, 59.

[208] Hebrews 11:6.

[209] Lewis, The Complete CS Lewis, 59.

[210] 2 Corinthians 5:21.

[211] Matthew 20:15.

[212] Consider Adam & Eve in the garden. God asks them, "Who told you that you were naked?" There was no one around to tell them they sinned, yet within themselves they knew. Because that part of them made to be like God was stirred. On this point, see Louie Giglio, Victory sermon series, February 2020, message 1.

[213] Galatians 1:9 As we have said before, so I say again now, if any man is preaching to you a gospel contrary to what you received, he is to be accursed! On rebuilding what he once destroyed, see Galatians 2:18.

[214] Romans 10:3.

[215] Hebrews 8:6–13, 9:11–10:18.

[216] Galatians 1:4. "He gave himself for our sins so that He might rescue us from this present evil age, according to the will of our God and Father …"

[217] Colossians 1:13.

[218] Luke 12:32.

[219] 2 Corinthians 4:4.

220 He tells us to pray His will be done on earth as it is in heaven in Matthew 6:10.

221 Philippians 4:11–12.

222 Philippians 1:21.

223 See Philippians 4:13.

224 2 Timothy 3:12 (ESV).

225 Romans 8:35–39.

226 Ephesians 2:5.

227 Colossians 2:13.

228 Ephesians 2:10

229 Colossians 1:10

230 "Poem" is the linguistic derivative of Paul's choice of Greek word for "workmanship."

231 Ephesians 3:11.

232 The gospel was completed by Christ's death and resurrection.

233 John 10:11,15.

234 John 10:17–18 (HCS).

235 John 19:30 (HCS).

236 John 15:13 (HCS).

237 I John 3:16 (HCS).

238 1 Peter 1:20, Revelation 13:8.

239 Psalm 139:16.

240 See John 2:9–10.

241 Matthew 26:29, also Luke 22:18. Drinking wine in the kingdom will mark a celebration.

242 Matthew 11:28–30.

243 2 Corinthians 3:18 (MSG).

244 2 Corinthians 3:18 (TPT).

245 2 Peter 1:3-10.

246 2 Timothy 3:17.

247 2 Corinthians 4:16–18.

248 Galatians 5:1

249 John 8:36

250 1 Peter 2:16

251 Exodus 1:8.

252 Exodus 7:5–6.

253 God's promise on the nature of the land is in Exodus 3:7–8.

254 Numbers 13:27.

[255] Numbers 13:28 (HCS).

[256] Numbers 13:30 (HCS).

[257] Exodus 13:32 (HCS).

[258] Numbers 13:33.

[259] Numbers 14:3.

[260] Numbers 14:7–9 (HCS).

[261] Numbers 14:11 (HCS).

[262] Numbers 14:20–23 (HCS).

[263] Numbers 14:24 (HCS).

[264] Numbers 14:28 (HCS).

[265] Genesis 2:19.

[266] Proverbs 18:21.

[267] Deuteronomy 6:10–12.

[268] Deuteronomy 6:20–25.

[269] Ezra 9:9 (HCS). The whole prayer is Ezra 9:6–15.

[270] Nehemiah 9:36 (HCS).

[271] Nehemiah 9:36–37 (HCS).

[272] Matthew 1:21 (HCS).

[273] Luke 4:17–19 (HCS).

[274] Luke 4:20–21 (HCS).

[275] John 8:36 (TPT).

[276] Romans 5:12, 17–18 (HCS).

[277] Romans 5:21.

[278] Romans 6:6-7 (HCS).

[279] Romans 7

[280] Romans 6:18–23.

[281] John 1:12, Galatians 4:5

[282] Ephesians 2:12–13 is clear that we were "far off," and 1 Peter 2:10 says we were once not a people, but are now the People of God.

[283] John 1:12–13 and 3:3–8.

[284] Romans 8:15 (TPT).

[285] Ephesians 1:5-6 (NKJV).

[286] Romans 8:1-2 (NAS 1995).

[287] Romans 8:15 (NAS 1995).

[288] Romans 8:21 (HCS).

[289] Romans 8:23 (NAS 1995).

[290] Galatians 4:5 (NAS 1995).

[291] Ephesians 1:5 (NAS 1995).

[292] Luke 15:16 (NAS 1995).

[293] Luke 15:19 (NAS 1995).

[294] Luke 15:21.

[295] Luke 15:24 (HCS).

[296] Galatians 3:27–29 (HCS).

[297] Galatians 4:4–7 (HCS).

[298] Ephesians 1:5 He predestined us to adoption as sons through Jesus Christ to Himself, according to the kind intention of His will.

[299] Deuteronomy 1:31 (HCS).

[300] Deuteronomy 8:5 (HCS).

[301] Deuteronomy 14:1 (HCS).

[302] Deuteronomy 32:6 (HCS).

[303] Isaiah 43:6–7.

[304] Isaiah 45:11.

[305] Jeremiah 31:9.

[306] Galatians 4:4.

[307] John 16:11, Jesus says "and about judgment, because the ruler of this world has been judged."

[308] 1 Peter 4:10 says "Based on the gift each one has received, use it to serve others, as good managers of the varied grace of God." (HCS)

[309] 1 Peter 5:8.

[310] Luke 10:19.

[311] 2 Corinthians 5:14–15, 17–21 (HCS).

[312] 2 Corinthians 5:15.

[313] 1 Peter 2:9.

[314] 2 Timothy 2:3–4.

[315] Meltzer and Mensch, The First Conspiracy: The Secret Plot to Kill George Washington, New York City: Flatiron Books. 356.

[316] Ibid, 356. It is said that Washington went home to Mount Vernon after six years of the war, and then not again until the eight years were up.

[317] Ibid, 356.

[318] Meltzer, 324–25.

[319] Ephesians 2:1–5.

[320] Even King David says the redemption of a soul is costly, and the price cannot be paid by riches. See Psalm 49:8. 1 Peter 1:18–19 says redemption required the blood of Jesus.

[321] Hebrews 12:2 (NAS 1995).

[322] Hebrews 2:14, "that through death He might render powerless him who had the power of death, that is, the devil." (NAS 1995)

[323] The word for contrary is used to say the winds were contrary to sailing the ship in Acts 27:4. Also, of Paul doing things in opposition to the name of Jesus in persecuting believers, Acts 26:9.

[324] The only other occurrence of the term in the New Testament is Matthew 1:19, where Joseph, not wishing to disgrace (to make a show of) Mary publicly, desires to act privately.

[325] Keener, Craig. The IVP Bible Background Commentary. Downers Grove, IVP, p574. Also "Roman Triumph." *Wikipedia*, Wikimedia Foundation, 23 Apr. 2021, en.wikipedia.org/wiki/Roman_triumph.

[326] 1 Corinthians 15:26, 27.

[327] 1 Corinthians 15:57.

[328] 1 John 3:8. See also Acts 10:38, that Jesus healed all under the tyranny of the devil, for God was with Him.

[329] Genesis 3:15.

[330] Revelation 1:14–18.

[331] Revelation 3:21 (HCS).

[332] Revelation 5:5 (HCS).

[333] 2 Peter 1:3 (HCS).

[334] Romans 8:37.

[335] Matthew 13:44.

[336] Ephesians 4:1.

[337] Hebrews 9:28 states a reason for His "second coming" to earth. "So also the Messiah, having been offered once to bear the sins of many, will appear a second time, not to bear sin, but to bring salvation to those who are waiting for Him."

[338] Luke 21:25–28 (ESV). See also Revelation 3:11, 1 Corinthians 4:5.

[339] Hebrews 10:23–25 (NAS1995) "Let us hold fast the confession of our hope without wavering, for He who promised is faithful; and let us consider how to stimulate one another to love and good deeds, not forsaking our own assembling together, as is the habit of some, but encouraging *one another;* and all the more as you see the day drawing near."

[340] Luke 23:41.

[341] Luke 23:42.

[342] Luke 23:43. This has parallel in the centurion story in Matthew 8:8–13. As the centurion exercises faith in who Jesus is, Jesus honors his faith.

[343] Luke 23:39–43.

[344] 2 Corinthians 5:20.

[345] Paul says of Abraham in Romans 4:18, "in hope against hope believed." Even when circumstances give no reason for hope, it can and should still be exercised.

[346] John 14:9.

[347] John 8:32.

[348] See 2 Tim 3:12, Phil 2:14–16.

[349] Galatians 1:11–24.

[350] 2 Corinthians 11:23–28.

[351] Acts 20:22–24, 27.

[352] Paul says he wants to know the fellowship of His sufferings. See Philippians 3:10.

[353] Colossians 4:3 (NAS1995) says that Paul asks for prayer that he "may speak forth the mystery of Christ, for which I have also been imprisoned."

[354] 2 Timothy 2:3, 9–10, 12. "Suffer hardship with *me* … I suffer hardship even to imprisonment as a criminal … For this reason I endure all things for the sake of those who are chosen … If we endure, we will also reign with Him."

[355] 2 Timothy 3:1–5, 10–17.

[356] Ephesians 6:20.

[357] Philippians 2:12–17.

[358] Nordeman, Nichole. "Dear Me." *Every Mile Mattered*, Sparrow Records, 2017, Track 3.

[359] Matthew 25:35–45.

[360] Matthew 5:14–16.

[361] John 3:19–20

[362] Romans 8:21b–25.

[363] Among the top grossing films of all time, *Titanic, Lord of the Rings, Beauty and the Beast*, and *Black Panther*, all exhibit some version of a redemption story.

[364] Galatians 6:9–10.

[365] Ephesians 4:22–24.

[366] Colossians 3:9–11.

367 Ephesians 6:10–11.

368 Paul sees God working in us mightily as an established promise in Colossians 1:29.

369 2 Corinthians 2:14–17.

370 Philippians 3:7–8.

371 Christians were called The Way in Acts 9:2; 19:9, 23; 22:4; 24:14, 22. Acts 8:1 says Paul agreed to Stephen's death.

372 1 Timothy 1:15-16 (HCS).

373 Ephesians 4:1.

374 Psalm 118:17 (HCS).

375 Romans 4:17–21 (TPT).

376 Romans 3:4 (HCS).

377 John 14:2–3. See 1 Corinthians 2:9, quoting Isaiah 64, the uniqueness of what we will experience.

378 Buechner, Frederick. Telling the Truth: The Gospel as Tragedy, Comedy, & Fairy Tale, Harper & Row, 1977, p.70.

379 Adam is the transliteration of the Hebrew word for man.

380 2 Corinthians 5:21 (TPT).

381 Philippians 2:12–13.

382 Galatians 3:14, 18, Ephesians 2:16, Hebrews 9:22.

383 2 Corinthians 5:14–21 (NAS 1995).

384 1 Peter 4:12,13.

385 Revelation 12:10–17.

386 1 Corinthians 15:57 "But thanks be to God, who gives us the victory through our Lord Jesus Christ."

387 Revelation 12:10–11 (NAS 1995).

388 Acts 20:24.

389 Acts 27:20.

390 Acts 27:22–25 (TPT).

391 Acts 20:24.

392 Acts 28:3–6. The Message translation says Paul was "no worse for the wear."

393 Revelation 21:5–8. Emphasis mine.

394 2 Timothy 1:7.

395 Acts 9:31. The word for fear here is phobos. It is not the same as in 2 Timothy 1:7 or Revelation 21:8.

396 Washer, Micha'el. When All The Pictures Are Restored. Master's Design Publishing.

[397] Romans 5:14. See also Hebrews 10:1 about shadow and reality.

[398] Revelation 22:1–7, 12-19 (NAS 1995).

[399] Revelation 22:2.

[400] The question of the survival of the tree of life in Eden after the flood is valid. Some points for study are found in "Questions about the Tree of Life." Bodie Hodge, 5/18/10. https://answersingenesis. org/garden-of-eden/questions- about-the-tree-of-life/

[401] Ezekiel 47:1-12 describes this.

[402] The Hebrew term is "beit hamidrash." I Kings 8:17–19 says Solomon will build a house for God's name. Solomon's temple was a "holy temple." In John 2:19–21, Jesus equates himself with temple, as a biblical "type," or foreshadowing for those redeemed by Jesus being the dwelling place of God.

[403] Revelation 22:14.

[404] Just as the Father in Luke 15 put on his son a robe and a ring, so the heavenly Father gives us "washed robes" and in doing this, *restores us to what we had in the beginning*, the Tree of Life.

[405] Genesis 3:23–24. "Therefore the LORD God sent him out from the garden of Eden, to cultivate the ground from which he was taken. So He drove the man out; and at the east of the garden of Eden He stationed the cherubim and the flaming sword which turned every direction to guard the way to the tree of life."

[406] Revelation 2:7.

[407] Revelation 3:4–5.

[408] Revelation 21:2–7.

[409] Revelation 22:17 (NAS 1995). The HCS says "whoever desires should take the living water as a gift."

[410] Revelation 22:20.

[411] MacDonald, George. "Life," Your Life in Christ. Edited by Michael Phillips. Bloomington: Bethany House, p.71. Essay is from MacDonald's "Unspoken Sermons."

[412] John 10:10 says, "The thief comes only to steal and kill and destroy; I came so that they would have life, and have *it* abundantly." 1 John 3:8 says, "The Son of God appeared for this purpose, to destroy the works of the devil."

[413] Matthew 16:24–27.

[414] 2 Peter 1:5–8 (ESV).

[415] Colossians 3:10.

[416] We are, in the words of Romans 13:14, putting on Christ, and making no provision for the flesh.

[417] Ephesians 4:3.

[418] Ephesians 4:4–6.

[419] Romans 12:1.

[420] 1 Peter 1:13–19.

[421] 1 John 2:25–28.

[422] Revelation 3:8, 12–13.

[423] Romans 16:25–27.

[424] Jude 24, 25.